FIGHTING DISINFORMATION ONLINE

Building the Database of Web Tools

JENNIFER KAVANAGH | SAMANTHA CHERNEY

HILARY REININGER | NORAH GRIFFIN

Sponsored by the William and Flora Hewlett Foundation

For more information on this publication, visit www.rand.org/t/RR3000

Library of Congress Cataloging-in-Publication Data is available for this publication.
ISBN: 978-1-9774-0430-5

Published (2020) by the RAND Corporation, Santa Monica, Calif.

RAND® is a registered trademark.

Cover images: Julien Eichinger/stock.adobe.com and Vladimir_Timofeev/gettyimages.com
Cover design by Pete Soriano

The RAND Corporation is a research organization that develops solutions to public policy challenges to help make communities throughout the world safer and more secure, healthier and more prosperous. RAND is nonprofit, nonpartisan, and committed to the public interest.

RAND's publications do not necessarily reflect the opinions of its research clients and sponsors.

Support RAND
Make a tax-deductible charitable contribution at
www.rand.org/giving/contribute

www.rand.org

Preface

Today's information ecosystem brings access to seemingly infinite amounts of information instantaneously, but it also creates challenges, such as the rapid spread of misinformation and disinformation to millions of people. In response to the challenge of online disinformation and as part of the RAND Corporation's Truth Decay initiative with support from the Hewlett Foundation, RAND researchers worked to identify and characterize the universe of online tools, created by nonprofit or civil society organizations, that target online disinformation. The purpose of the project was three-fold. First, we sought to identify and collect in one place a set of resources to help users combat the challenge of disinformation and gain greater awareness of the media ecosystem. Second, we intended that the database be used to inform funders and developers about the set of tools under development, those tools in need of funding, and areas where additional development would be beneficial. Third, we aimed to provide a map of ongoing projects and developed tools that could support efforts to build a field around the study of disinformation. This report summarizes the data collected by the RAND team in 2018 and 2019 and serves as a companion to the web database (www.rand.org/research/projects/truth-decay/fighting-disinformation).

This report is one of a series that focuses on the topic of Truth Decay. The original report, *Truth Decay: An Initial Exploration of the Diminishing Role of Facts and Analysis in American Public Life* by Jennifer Kavanagh and Michael D. Rich, was published in January 2018 and laid out a research agenda for studying and developing solutions to the Truth Decay challenge.

This study was undertaken by RAND Education and Labor, a division of the RAND Corporation that conducts research on early childhood through postsecondary education programs, workforce development, and programs and policies affecting workers, entrepreneurship, and financial literacy and decisionmaking.

Funding

Funding for this research was provided by a grant from the William and Flora Hewlett Foundation.

Contents

Figures and Tables

Figures

Tables

Summary

Today's information ecosystem brings both promise and challenges. On the one hand, people have access to an increasing amount of information instantaneously and at low cost. On the other, the Internet and social media facilitate the rapid spread of misinformation and disinformation to millions of people. In response to the challenge of online disinformation—and as part of the RAND Corporation's Truth Decay initiative with support from the Hewlett Foundation[1]—RAND researchers worked to identify and characterize the universe of online tools, created by nonprofit or civil society organizations, that target online disinformation. The purpose of the project was three-fold:

1. We sought to identify and collect in one place a set of resources that can help users combat the challenge of disinformation, gain greater awareness of the media ecosystem, and become more-informed media consumers.
2. We intended that the database be used to inform funders and tool developers about the set of tools already under development, those tools in need of funding, and areas where additional focused efforts would be beneficial.

---

[1] *Truth Decay* is the term we are using to refer to the diminishing role of facts, data, and analysis in political and civil discourse and the policymaking process. Truth Decay is characterized by four trends: increasing disagreement about facts and data, blurring of the line between opinion and fact, increasing relative volume of opinion compared with fact, and declining trust in institutions that used to be looked to as authoritative sources of factual information.

3. We aimed to provide a map of ongoing projects and developed tools that could support efforts to build a field around the study of disinformation and its remedies.

This report summarizes the data collected by the RAND team in 2018 and 2019 and serves as a companion to the already published web database.[2] The report provides information on our inclusion and exclusion criteria (which types of tools are the focus of the data set), a discussion of methodology, a list of domains or characteristics that we coded for every tool (e.g., tool type, delivery platform), a summary of descriptive statistics that provides multiple different snapshots of the available tools and tools in development, and a series of deep dives that describe each of the types of tools in the database and how each works to counter the disinformation challenge.

How We Chose the Tools in This Database

Each tool listed in this database aims to improve the online information ecosystem in some way, such as by shaping the way that information is shared or by providing tools that allow information consumers to better navigate the media and information sources with which they interact. We identified tools through web searches, articles that review tools and advances in this field, and discussions with experts (e.g., those involved in developing or funding tools). For each tool, we collected and provided as much information as possible, but it was rare that we were able to fill in every field for a given tool. We used several inclusion and exclusion criteria:

1. **Each entry is a tool or platform that either is interactive or provides some product that consumers can use or apply to their own web-browsing or information consumption.** This means that online games, courses, image verification platforms,

---

[2] RAND Corporation, "Fighting Disinformation Online: A Database of Web Tools," webpage, 2019.

and disinformation trackers would be featured, but websites that offer general-purpose resources would not be.

2. **This database is focused on tools developed by nonprofit and civil society organizations.** One of our goals for the database was that it would provide a more complete picture of the set of tools available in this space and of the gaps that exist. This information will be useful to the general public and to researchers and philanthropic organizations looking to make the most productive investment of available resources. As a result, each entry must be produced or disseminated by a nonprofit entity. We exclude products developed by for-profit companies or tools developed for commercial purposes.

3. **Each entry must be explicitly focused on online disinformation.** There are some tools—such as many ad blockers and other privacy tools—that could serve a counter-disinformation purpose, even if this is not their primary function. In our database, we include only tools that explicitly reference disinformation as the target of the tool.

4. **We focused on U.S.-based tools targeting the U.S. market,** but many of the tools are applied internationally.

Describing the Tools

We identified a total of 79 tools that fit the criteria (as of August 2019). We coded each tool on a number of dimensions, such as its type, method, origin, focus, and how it was funded. Here, we provide details on each of the categories and key insights that emerged from our analysis of the database.

Type of Tool

We have identified seven types of tools, and each tool is classified into at least one (and up to two) of the categories (Table S.1). The seven types are as follows:

1. **Bot and spam detection:** This refers to tools intended to identify automated accounts on social media platforms. There are

Table S.1
Tool Type Frequencies

Tool Type	Frequency
Bot and spam detection	3
Credibility-scoring	14
Codes and standards	5
Disinformation tracking	6
Verification	45
Whitelisting	5
Education and training	20
TOTAL	98

many challenges associated with detecting bots—not only are there far too many for any one actor to identify, but bot programmers also adapt quickly to evade detection. Third-party organizations might never have the ability to remove content from a social media platform. But, by flagging bots, they might be able to address some piece of the challenge or at least provide information about content origin for users navigating online.

2. **Credibility-scoring:** This category of tools comprises those that attach a rating or grade to individual sources based on their accuracy, quality, or trustworthiness. Credibility-scoring initiatives also vary in their format (e.g., browser extension, website, or app) and the details of how they work, but all attempt to classify and categorize information sources to help better inform user decisions about media consumption.

3. **Codes and standards:** There are several types of codes and standards. All stem from the creation of a set of principles or processes that members must commit and adhere to in return for some outward sign of membership that can be recognized by others. Some of these tools focus on news producers, setting standards for journalists or news outlets or organizations; others target news consumers with a set of desired behaviors. These tools do not rate credibility or accuracy, nor do they verify or

fact-check information. Tools vary in the extent to which they have mechanisms to hold members accountable for the commitments made and the types of monitoring conducted.

4. **Disinformation tracking:** This applies to tools that track and/ or study the flow and prevalence of disinformation. A disinformation tracker literally tracks disinformation, either tracking specific pieces of disinformation and their spread over time or measuring or reporting the level of fake or misleading news on a particular platform.

5. **Verification:** This applies to fact-checking tools that aim to ascertain the accuracy of information and tools that work to authenticate photos, images, and other information. There are many types of verification tools, such as those that work using artificial intelligence (AI) and those that rely on human implementation. Verification is a necessary part of the fight against disinformation, but evidence is mixed regarding its ability to change people's minds. Furthermore, the amount of disinformation in the information ecosystem far exceeds the capacity of fact-checking tools, and these tools typically require an engaged user who is interested in identifying what is factual.

6. **Whitelisting:** These tools create trusted lists of internet protocol (IP) addresses or websites to distinguish between trusted users or trusted sites and ones that might be fake or malicious.

7. **Education and training:** This applies to any courses, games, and activities aimed at combating disinformation by teaching individuals new skills or concepts. We list only online courses, games, and activities that have an interactive component; a traditional, classroom-based curriculum likely would not be featured, but an online training would be. In theory, media literacy education (including online games and activities) holds promise as a tool against disinformation. If individuals are better able to separate fact from opinions or fiction, to assess the credibility of sources, to identify disinformation, and to search for and find facts when they need them, they might be less susceptible to disinformation campaigns. The question is, do these programs work? To date, we do not have the information needed to make this assessment.

Method

We also characterized tools based on the method or technology they use. The most common method used by disinformation tools in the database is *machine learning and AI*. About one-third of tools use some sort of automated method, whether an algorithm to identify bots and spam or some form of AI to detect when the metadata of photos or videos have been manipulated. The second most common method is *human implementation*. This is the simplest method and can be implemented with few start-up costs, but it is also time intensive and requires extensive human effort. As a result, these efforts might be harder to scale. The third most common method used by disinformation tools is to develop and promote *online courses and games*. Later, we will demonstrate that this method is almost exclusively used with one tool type (education and training). Other methods, such as the use of *blockchain technology* and *crowdsourcing*, are less frequent overall but common among some of the newer tools. Crowdsourcing, for example, relies on the collective opinions of users to verify the accuracy of information and assess source credibility. This method costs less and is less time-consuming than human implementation methods, but it assumes that average users can accurately assess source credibility and information accuracy and that this accurate information will rise to the top.[3] Table S.2 lists the tools by primary technology or method.

Other Characteristics

We also capture information on several other aspects of the tools and study patterns and trends.

- **Intended audience:** Tools we identified target the general public most often, and were also aimed at journalists, researchers, and teachers.
- **Tool status and date of origin:** We provide information on the level of maturity of the tool, whether it is fully operational

---

[3] On challenges of crowdsourcing, see, for example, Scott Clement and Callum Borchers, "Facebook Plans to Crowdsource Media Credibility. This Chart Shows Why That Will Be So Difficult," *Washington Post*, January 24, 2018.

Table S.2
Frequency of Tool Methods

Method Type	Frequency
Machine learning and AI	27
Human implementation	22
Online course or game	19
Crowdsourcing	8
Blockchain	3
TOTAL	79

or in some form of testing. Most tools in the database are fully operational.

- **Degree of automation:** This captures whether the tool operates on its own (through an app or other mechanism) or requires human implementation. We found that a large number of tools continue to rely on human implementation, which constrains scalability.
- **Delivery:** We considered whether tools are delivered by website, web extension, mobile app, or another way. Although mobile technologies are becoming increasingly common and widespread, most tools in the database rely primarily on websites or extensions.
- **Tool focus:** We explored whether the tool focuses on content (the actual disinformation after publication) or the process by which that information is produced and shared. Although more than one-half of our tools focus on content, those that focus on process might be better able to stop disinformation before it is shared.
- **Theory of change:** This field provides a brief description of how the tool fights disinformation. The majority of tools fall into one of two categories: They focus either on improving the quality of information available or on providing individuals with skills to better navigate the information system.
- **Connection with tech platforms:** This field describes how—if at all—a tool is connected to technology platforms, such as Google, Twitter, and Facebook. The connection could be funding, partnership, or formal adoption of the tool by the platform.

- **Funding source:** We provide a list of organizations, foundations, and/or individuals that fund the tool, based on publicly available information. Almost all tools have more than one source of funding. Civil society organizations are the primary funders of tools, followed by commercial and government funders.
- **External evaluations:** Most tools did not have formal evaluations.

Future Directions and Gaps to Be Addressed

Our review of tools highlights several gaps and priority areas of growth and investments when it comes to the field of online, civil society–developed tools to counter disinformation.

Need for Rigorous Evaluations

Throughout our review of tools, we were interested in finding objective evaluations of the extent to which the tools identified in our database had been proven effective in the fight against disinformation. In general, these evaluations were not publicly available, if they existed at all. In an ideal world, investment dollars, grants, and contributions to civil society organizations working to counter disinformation should be allocated based on efficacy. Tools that prove able to reliably counter the spread of disinformation or to improve individual resilience to disinformation should be the ones to receive continued funding and support. Without such metrics, funders are left without an objective criterion on which to make investment decisions. There are reasons for this gap, such as the frequently high costs of such evaluations and the fact that it might be difficult to create realistic use environments in which to conduct evaluations for some tools. However, to the extent possible, **civil society tools profiled in this database should be rigorously evaluated using assessments and longitudinal analysis based on randomized control trials.** Such an investment could then inform the future direction of the field because subsequent investment could be allocated toward types of tools (or even specific tools) that, based on objective data, seem to hold the most promise as counters to disinformation.

Invest in Automation and Applications

One of the biggest obstacles that civil society organizations face when developing tools to counter online disinformation is their ability to scale the tool—getting a sufficiently large population of people to use the tool and then developing the capability needed to support the tool at a larger scale. One productive set of investments might focus on supporting the ability of existing tools to reach and serve larger audiences by focusing on expanding delivery methods and committing to automation. First, the ability to increase a tool's scale and reach will depend on accessibility and usability. The tools in our database had three primary modes of delivery—websites, browser extensions, and apps. Only a small number of tools in this database used mobile apps. Mobile apps are highly portable and easily integrated into the information consumption habits of users. **Investments focused on the development of mobile applications for existing tools might therefore increase the user base of certain tools**. Development of apps and tablet versions of tools might also facilitate use in classrooms. However, not all tools can be built into applications (for example, bot-detection tools or disinformation trackers would be difficult to build into a mobile application). **Other alternatives to increase scale could be partnerships across tools or between tools and browsers to make built-in versions of extensions, or at least make available extensions more visible. Support for marketing and outreach might also be beneficial.** Importantly, not all tools are built to be scaled. Instead, some tools are intended for very specialized audiences but still add value.

Second, the ability of a civil society organization to support an expanded user base is dependent on the method used by the tool. Such methods as machine learning, AI, crowdsourcing, and blockchain can be much more scalable because they are either automated or less labor-intensive. However, these technologies remain somewhat undeveloped as applied to online tools. For example, machine learning and AI have been applied, to some extent, to support verification tools, but accuracy could be improved. For such technologies as machine learning, AI, crowdsourcing, and blockchain, any improvements in accuracy, delivery, ease of use, and reliability would be valuable across the field and could support a more widespread user base in the fight against disinformation.

Acknowledgments

Many people contributed to the writing of this report. We would like to thank Kelly Born and Daniel Stid and the Madison Initiative at the William and Flora Hewlett Foundation for the generous support that made this report and the accompanying online database possible. We are also grateful to Ben Scott and Elizabeth Bodine-Baron for their helpful reviews and feedback throughout the project that made the final products better.

At RAND, we also thank Fatih Unlu for his contributions to the report and his assistance in revising and refining the final products, and Shanthi Nataraj for her excellent guidance throughout the project. We are also appreciative of the efforts made by our colleagues who assisted in the development of the database that accompanies this report, including Deanna Lee, Alyson Youngblood, and Lee Floyd, as well as Shawn Smith, who assisted in the collection of the underlying data. Arwen Bicknell edited the document.

CHAPTER ONE

Introduction

The rise of the Internet and the advent of social media have fundamentally changed the information ecosystem. Many of these changes have been decidedly positive. Consumers now have more access to more information with no wait time and often with less filter than in the past. Put another way, access to information has been democratized. Consumers do not have to wait for the evening broadcast news, in which information is packaged and distilled; they can access information instantaneously and often directly from the source or through multiple sources. However, the ubiquitous access to information has also created new challenges. Most notably, with so much information and so many sources of it, distinguishing between good information and low-quality or false information is often nearly impossible. Social media, in fact, makes the spread of false and misleading information significantly easier than it was in the past. Before social media was prevalent, an individual or organization who decided to spread disinformation was limited by the number of people he or she could talk to or interact with; now, anyone can spread false information to millions of people with one click of a button. Disinformation thus spreads further and faster online than it ever could have hoped to in another format. At the same time, an increasing number of people are turning to social media or other online platforms to seek out news about the world, the nation, and their communities.[1]

---

[1] For more discussion of this problem, see Jennifer Kavanagh and Michael D. Rich, *Truth Decay: An Initial Exploration of the Diminishing Role of Facts and Analysis in American Public Life*, Santa Monica, Calif.: RAND Corporation, RR-2314-RC, 2018.

Alina Polyakova offers a helpful metaphor for explaining the effect of disinformation online—its pervasiveness and reach—by inviting us to "imagine a pool of water. That pool of water is our public discourse. And you drop into that pool of water a drop of ink, and at first you see the origin, you see the source. But very quickly it dissipates, it becomes part of the mainstream, and you no longer know what is true and what is fake, what is a lie and what is reality, and that is the purpose of a disinformation campaign."[2] Although it is hard to get good data on the volume of false information online, past research suggests that much of the American public has been exposed to some sort of disinformation online, be it political or on some other topic.[3]

The challenge of disinformation can be addressed through multiple means: There are policy and regulatory responses from the government, efforts by the tech companies themselves to self-police, initiatives by for-profit companies to build programs and tools that counter or detect disinformation, and similar projects by nonprofit organizations to develop tools, games, and other interventions that counter the spread of disinformation. Interventions that fall into these latter two categories are particularly interesting. Regulatory or policy changes are likely to occur slowly and with significant debate; interventions that operate at the level of the information producer or consumer can be implemented more quickly, are less likely to encounter resistance and roadblocks, and can more directly affect the behavior of individuals and the quality of information available.

The difference between for-profit and nonprofit tools and interventions is also important, however. For-profit tools are developed with the purpose of earning a profit; thus, development is geared toward efforts likely to make money, and results are available only to those willing and able to pay. This limits the reach—and, potentially—the effect of such tools. However, the availability of a funding stream (subscription or purchase costs) also allows these companies to continue to invest and develop their interventions and

---

[2] Atlantic Council, "Why Should We Care About Disinformation?" YouTube, June 9, 2017.

[3] Hunt Allcott, Matthew Gentzkow, and Chuan Yu, "Trends in the Diffusion of Misinformation on Social Media," *Research & Politics*, Vol. 6, No. 2, April-June 2019.

to market them widely. Nonprofits often have more-constrained resources, which limits investment or slows development. Nonprofits also might lack the platform needed to publicize or launch tools, or they might struggle to achieve a scale at which tools or programs become self-sustaining or have the expected effect. However, tools from nonprofits are also likely to be more widely accessible—for example, to an average user who might be unable to pay for a tool that comes with an upfront cost. Most tools created by nonprofits have no cost, or at least a no-cost version, and are meant to be downloaded and used by individual users without substantial external support. Nonprofit tools are generally among the more innovative—nonprofit developers often make use of cutting-edge methodologies, are willing to experiment with new applications, and tackle complicated problems in unique ways. For all of these reasons, nonprofit interventions targeting the disinformation challenge are likely to be central to the development and implementation of a solution.

As disinformation has spread, and as attention to the resulting challenge has increased, the variety of nonprofit tools and interventions has increased as well. This is certainly a positive development. However, there has been little effort to coordinate across these products and little effort to document the variety of different tools, games, and other interventions that are available; how they work; and whom they target. This lack of information creates three problems. First, users might struggle with determining what is available or choosing the right tool for their needs. Second, funders, seeking to support nonprofit developers, might not have a clear view of which tools show the highest potential for success or where additional investment might be needed. Finally, developers interested in building new tools might not know which markets are saturated or where there is room for new interventions. This report and the online database it describes attempt to address this lack of coordination by documenting the variety of tools available and providing basic information on each as a way to guide decisions and choices of users, developers, and funders.

Objective of This Report

In response to this urgent need and as part of the RAND Corporation's Truth Decay initiative and with support from the Hewlett Foundation,[4] RAND researchers worked to identify and characterize the universe of online tools, created by nonprofit or civil society organizations, that target online disinformation. The purpose of the project was three-fold. First, we sought to identify and collect a set of resources that can help users combat the challenge of disinformation, gain greater awareness of the media ecosystem, and become more-informed media consumers. Second, we intended that the database be used to inform funders and developers about the set of tools under development, those tools in need of funding, and areas where additional development would be beneficial. Third, we aimed to provide a map of ongoing projects and developed tools that could support efforts to build a field around the study of disinformation and its remedies.

This report summarizes the data collected by the RAND team in 2018 and 2019 and serves as a companion to the already published web database.[5] This report provides information on our inclusion and exclusion criteria (which types of tools are the focus of the data set), a discussion of methodology, a list of domains or characteristics that we coded for every tool (e.g., tool type, delivery platform), a summary of descriptive statistics that provides multiple different snapshots of the available tools and tools in development, and a series of deep dives describing tools that appear to have particular promise for countering the disinformation challenge. This report describes the data as they were at the point of publication, in database form, in November 2019. Because the data are being updated on a rolling basis, the database has evolved and will continue to do so.

---

[4] *Truth Decay* is the term we are using to refer to the diminishing role of facts, data, and analysis in political and civil discourse and the policymaking process. Truth Decay is characterized by four trends: increasing disagreement about facts and data, blurring of the line between opinion and fact, increasing relative volume of opinion compared with fact, and declining trust in institutions that used to be looked to as authoritative sources of factual information. See Kavanagh and Rich, 2018.

[5] RAND Corporation, "Fighting Disinformation Online: A Database of Web Tools," webpage, 2019.

CHAPTER TWO

Approach and Definitions

As noted in Chapter One, we focused our attention on online disinformation and tools developed by nonprofits to confront the challenges it poses. In this chapter, we provide detailed information on how we located tools, how we determined what to include or exclude, and how we collected information about the tools featured in our database. We identify each of the dimensions used in our assessment and the rationale for using that dimension (why that information could be helpful in evaluating or reviewing tools).

Identifying Tools

To identify tools for inclusion, we relied on several sources. First, we reviewed previous mapping exercises carried out by others in the field, including maps developed by the Credibility Coalition and by the Hewlett Foundation. These lists provided a wide variety of different kinds of tools and initiatives: Although not all of these tools fell within the scope of our analysis, the lists did provide a strong foundation on which to build. Second, we conducted web searches to identify additional tools and efforts that might warrant inclusion. These searches were structured around tool types, such as "fact-checking" or "credibility-scoring," as well as around more-general search terms, such as "disinformation tools" or "tools to counter disinformation." In addition to directly identifying tools, these searches often led us to tools indirectly, through review articles that summarize new innovations or new tools. Third, we discussed the state of the field with key researchers and funders. These individuals were able to identify newly initiated efforts and to provide guidance on specific types of tools or products that might warrant inclusion. These discussions were also useful for identifying specific tool characteristics or dimensions that warranted inclusion in our analysis and database. We stopped searching when we felt we had reached a point of saturation, but we recognize that this is a rapidly changing and evolving field and have built an easy mechanism through which the database can be updated. Data described in this report are current as of July 1, 2019.

Criteria for Inclusion

Our database focused on a particular set of tools, particularly those that target disinformation online with the intention of improving the online information ecosystem in some way, such as by shaping the way that information is shared or by providing tools with which information consumers can better navigate the media ecosystem.

We employed four primary inclusion and exclusion criteria. Only tools meeting these four criteria are featured in our database:

1   **Tools in our database must be interactive.** Each entry is a tool that either is interactive or produces something that the consumer is able to use or apply to their own web-browsing or information consumption. This means that online games, courses, image verification platforms, and disinformation trackers would be featured, but websites that offer general-purpose resources would not be. We also include fact-checking tools and platforms because these provide users with assessments of information quality and veracity.

2. **Tools in our database are created by nonprofits.** This database is focused on tools developed by nonprofit and civil society organizations. One goal we have for the database is that it provide a more complete picture of the set of tools available in this space and of the gaps that exist. This information will be useful to information consumers and to researchers and philanthropic organizations looking to make the most productive investment

of available resources. As a result, each entry must be produced or disseminated by a nonprofit entity. We exclude products of for-profit companies, even those that are free of cost. Note that not all tools created by nonprofits are free to the user.

3. **Tools in our database must have an explicit focus on disinformation.** Each entry must address online disinformation explicitly. Some tools, such as many ad blockers and other privacy tools, could serve a counter-disinformation purpose, even if this is not their primary function. However, we feature only those that explicitly reference disinformation as the target of the tool.

4. **Tools in our database are primarily focused on the U.S. market.** We centered our attention on U.S.-based tools targeting the U.S. market, but many of the tools are applied internationally. Future iterations of this database could include international tools.

Coding Tool Dimensions

For each tool identified in our database, we collected information on a variety of different dimensions. As noted, dimensions for inclusion were identified through discussions with the sponsor and interviews with funders and researchers to identify what they considered useful and interesting to know about new and emerging tool developments. To collect information on these tools, we again relied largely on web searches, analysis of tool websites or promotional materials, experimentation with the tools, reviews of articles written about the tools, and assessments and evaluations of the tools that were conducted by third parties.

In this section, we identify the full set of tool dimensions captured in our database. We provide information on how we coded each dimension and a rationale for why that dimension is in the database.

Founding Organization

This field captures the name of the organization behind the development of the tool. This can be useful in assessing the institutional backing behind the tool and assessing how the tool might be related to other available products.

Tool Name

This field captures the name of the tool.

Website

This field provides the weblink to the tool or information about the tool for those tools still in development.

Cost

We specify whether the tool has a cost or is free. Because we focus on nonprofits, the majority of products are free. However, there are several cases in which an organization provides both a free tool and, for a fee, a more advanced version. When this is the case, we provide this information. Understanding the cost of a tool is relevant for two reasons. First, it provides information about access to the tool. Tools that are free are more accessible than those that have an associated cost. Second, tools that charge fees for use have a very different funding model and thus might be less dependent on grants or contributions for survival. As noted elsewhere, we exclude free tools developed by for-profit companies.

Automation

This field captures whether the tool requires human implementation or functions automatically—for example, through the use of algorithms, machine learning, or artificial intelligence (AI). We also provide the option for mixed tools that combine more than one method. When considering the scalability of the tool and its ability to support mass distribution and use, automated tools are strongly preferred because they can support use at such a large scale. Tools that need to be updated or completed by humans (for example, fact-checking that requires analysis by individual fact-checkers or credibility-scoring that relies on human coders) will simply be too time-intensive to be widely scaled in terms of users or amount of media ecosystem covered. Human implementation also poses challenges in updating practices to reflect new information or new tools. In contrast, tools that have an automated mechanism can become self-sustaining once the necessary algorithms or processes are established. Crowdsourced tools exist at the intersection. These tools are certainly not automated in the sense of AI or machine learning, but they do not face the same bottlenecks as tools that must be implemented by one individual. Instead, crowdsourced tools rely on the aggregated input of many coders. These tools might be more difficult to scale than tools that rely solely on AI or machine learning, but they can be updated and adapted more easily than a tool that requires analysis or assessment by one individual.

Founder and Primary Contact
Where possible, we provide a primary contact for the tool, often the original developer or founder.

Delivery Platform
This field describes the means of delivery; that is, whether the tool is provided through an application, a website, a browser extension, a mobile application, a combination of these, or some other means. The delivery platform is relevant for a few reasons. First, understanding means of delivery can be valuable to users seeking out these tools. Second, different tools imply different ease of use and scalability. A tool that requires a user to download a browser extension or to visit a website has additional barriers to use because the user must seek out the tool and download or activate it for use. In contrast, tools that work through applications, although they still require some initiative on the part of the user, can be set up to be much more ingrained in the news consumption process of individual users. Moreover, as news and information consumption become increasingly mobile in nature, tools that can be delivered by mobile application will have much wider reach than tools that work only through websites or browser extensions.

Type of Tool
Different tools aim to do different things. We have identified seven types of tools:

1. **Bot and spam detection:** These tools are intended to identify automated accounts on social media platforms.
2. **Credibility-scoring:** These tools attach a rating or grade to individual sources based on their accuracy, quality, or trustworthiness.
3. **Codes and standards:** These are tools that establish new norms, principles, or best practices to govern a set of processes or to guide conduct and behavior. In the majority of the tools presented here, codes and standards aim to guard against disinformation or misinformation, to increase the quality of journalism, or to commit individuals or companies to a set of principles. There are several variations of codes and standards. One set is intended to guide the practices and products of journalists. Others are established to guide the behavior and habits of news consumers.[1]
4. **Disinformation tracking:** These are tools that track and/or study the flow and prevalence of disinformation.
5. **Verification:** This applies to fact-checking tools that aim to ascertain the accuracy of information.
6. **Whitelisting:** These tools create trusted lists of internet protocol (IP) addresses or websites to distinguish between trusted users or sites and ones that might be fake or malicious.
7. **Education and training:** This applies to any courses, games, and activities aimed at combating disinformation by teaching new skills or concepts to users and students. We provide only online courses, games, and activities that have an interactive component, so a traditional, classroom-based curriculum would likely not be featured, but an online training would be.

We classify each tool into at least one and up to two of these categories, with the primary tool type listed first. Classifying tools by type

---

[1] Codes and standards typically do not provide verification of the accuracy of information or assess credibility of information but instead create a set of standards; encourage journalists, newspapers, advertisers, or users to live up to those standards; and then provide an external marker of membership as a signal to others and an accountability mechanism.

is central to understanding the landscape of tools intended to counter disinformation.

A Note on Excluded Tool Types

There are several types of tools that are relevant to the challenge of online disinformation but that we intentionally exclude from our database because of their wider remit and their less direct ties with the disinformation issue. Here, we discuss these tools and how they relate to the disinformation challenge.

Ad Blockers

Ad blockers originated as tools that were narrowly built to block online advertisements. They typically work through the use of *blacklists*, which deny identified sites access to an individual or network, or *whitelists*, which let through only those sites that are on a preset list. These types of programs can be useful against disinformation because of what ads might bring with them: malware, disinformation, and an opportunity for companies to collect data on individuals who might click on those ads. By limiting access to individuals, ad blockers cut off a chain valuable to advertisers that contributes to microtargeting and facilitates the spread of disinformation. More recently, some ad blockers have taken the controversial step of allowing some companies preferred status, meaning that the ads of these companies are whitelisted and allowed through. Typically, ads have to meet some set of criteria before they are permitted this status, and individuals can choose to opt out of even these. We exclude these tools despite their potential use against disinformation because tackling the challenge of online disinformation is largely a secondary, often unacknowledged, benefit of these blockers, and the size of that benefit varies widely based on the nature of the tool and how it works. We include ad blockers that explicitly reference their disinformation application.

Privacy Tools

There are many different types of privacy tools available, but what they share is an interest in protecting users' personal data and online behavior so that individual users are not tracked online by malicious actors, their data is not stolen, and they are somewhat protected from microtargeting for ads and information. The most common privacy tools are virtual private networks (VPNs) and anonymization tools that disguise an individual's IP address and online behavior, searches, or location, protecting them from microtargeted ads or information and individualized content curation. As it pertains to disinformation, because they block cookie placement and ambient surveillance, the strongest privacy tools can prevent behavior profiling and the resulting organic content curation, and in doing so, might be able to undermine the basis of filter bubbles. We exclude these tools despite their potential use against disinformation because, like ad blockers, their addressing of the challenge of online disinformation is largely a secondary benefit, and the size of that benefit varies widely based on the nature of the tool and how it works. We include privacy tools that explicitly reference their disinformation application, and we encourage continued exploration of how privacy tools can and already do work against disinformation.

Commercial Media Monitoring

These tools are designed for corporations and offer services from brand management to social media analytics to cyber security. These tools do not meet the criteria for inclusion because they are for-profit and because their focus is on helping companies maintain and improve their reputation, maximize the effect of their advertising and social media campaigns, and ensure the security of their own information and systems. We acknowledge that these tools could be useful against disinformation in a few ways. First, corporations might not want their ads associated with disinformation and "fake news" sites. These commercial services can conduct some credibility-scoring of different websites to ensure that ads appear on verified sites. Second, commercial media monitors might identify instances of disinformation against a corporation—on social media or elsewhere, allowing for counter-messaging efforts. On the other hand, commercial media monitoring might contribute to the problem, if it allows corporations to improve their microtargeting efforts.

Free Tools Developed by For-Profit Companies

As noted, our database features only tools developed by nonprofit organizations and excludes even free tools developed by for-profit organizations. Some of these free tools have many of the same objectives as tools listed in the database—and, because they are free, they might be useful to information consumers. For example, NewsGuard offers a browser extension that provides a "Nutrition Label" for a large number of online news and information sites (more than 2,000, according to the organization). Each label offers an assessment of the accuracy, transparency, credibility, and quality of the information source. Similarly, Trusted News, owned by Factmata, uses a browser extension to provide users with information about the credibility, bias, and quality of news sources online. Both of these resources, then, are credibility-scoring tools similar in many ways to those in our database, except for the nature of their developer. In future iterations, we hope to be able to expand our efforts and capture these types of resources.

Tools Developed Internationally

The database focuses on tools developed within the United States and targeted at the U.S. market. This means that it excludes some tools developed internationally that might be useful to U.S.-based users. For example, Newswise by the Canadian organization CIVIX offers media literacy activities and videos, and it resembles many of the media literacy tools captured in our database. There are many other examples of valuable international tools, particularly in the area of media literacy. We hope to expand the data presented here to include those in the future.

Method Used by Tool

This field captures how the tool works; that is, the method or technique it uses to verify, track, identify, or score information. This is distinct from the tool type because although the tool type tells a user *what* the tool does, the method tells the user or other developers *how* the tool works. For example, our database includes fact-checking tools that work using crowd-sourcing and tools that rely on human implementation. The inclusion of this field allows us to distinguish between these different tools:

- **Blockchain:** This term means that tools use a shared and continuously updated record of virtual transactions to signal or record the credibility and accuracy of information to identify and build trust in true and accurate information.

- **Crowdsourcing:** These tools rely on user participation and engagement as a main element of their operating framework. This could mean efforts to establish the credibility of information or identify disinformation.
- **Human implementation:** Tools in this group require human implementation or action to complete; examples are fact-checking done by individuals and credibility-scoring operated by individuals.
- **Machine learning and AI:** These terms refer to tools that operate autonomously, using algorithms or other AI-driven processes. Examples are bot and spam detectors that use the behavior and profiles of identified accounts to identify bots.
- **Online course or game:** This applies to such tools as online interactive activities or web-based curricula that aim to educate or inform users about disinformation, how to detect disinformation, and how to mitigate disinformation.

Description of Tool

We provide a short description of the tool, what it does, and how it works. This information is essential for understanding and ultimately evaluating the tool.

Date Created

We provide the year in which the tool originated. Knowing how long a tool has been around is one way to assess its maturity but also gives a sense of how enduring it is or is likely to be. A tool that has already been around for a few years shows more "staying power" than a tool that is a month old. Although both might ultimately survive, we can have more confidence in the survivability of tools that have been around for a longer period of time.

Theory Behind the Tool

In this field, we discuss the rationale of each tool; that is, why developers believe that their tool will target disinformation online. This information is taken from the description of the tool and other relevant literature, such as white papers. Even tools with similar types and methods could have different theories of change in some instances, and different tools have different amounts of resources invested in developing a robust and complete theory of change. Developers that have spent more time mapping out and explaining their theory of change might produce tools that are more sophisticated and ultimately more effective at achieving their objectives. In our analysis, we broadly consider two types of tools, those for which the theory of change focuses on improving the quality of information available (e.g., verification), and those that instead focus on better training and preparing consumers to navigate the information environment and to distinguish between fact and falsehood.

Focused on Content vs. Process

Tools that are content-focused work by evaluating or analyzing information directly, whether it is the accuracy of a story or the authenticity of a photo. Tools that are focused on process consider how information is produced and disseminated. For example, fact-checking is based on a review of content; bot and spam detectors focus on process (patterns of information-sharing, followers, etc.). A smaller set of tools feature aspects of both. Both types of tools are necessary for countering online disinformation, but distinguishing between the two can be important. Tools that focus on process might have a deeper and more enduring effect in countering disinformation because they can help disrupt the dissemination of false or misleading information at the source. Content-based tools can correct inaccuracies but might not be able to sway users who have already made up their minds on an issue.

Funders

Where we could find information on sources of funding, we have provided it. Because the tools in this database are all developed by nonprofits, many tools have multiple sources of funding. This information is useful because it provides insight into which organizations or foundations are supporting which tools, which tools have private corporate backing, which are supported by a big tech platform, which by organizations involved in the news media, etc. In some cases, funding information was not available at the time we collected the initial data in 2018–2019.

Status (Maturity)

We assessed the level of development of each tool, with a variety of different options. Understanding how developed the tool is could be valuable for several reasons. First, this information can provide insight into the type of support the tool needs. A tool that is just getting off the ground might benefit from large infusions of funds, whereas tools that are already developed might need only steady maintenance. Second, the stage of development tells funders and others considering involvement the risk associated with investing in the tool. A tool that is fully developed and on the market will have much less risk associated with it than a tool just entering development or even one in early testing phases.

- **In development:** The tool is still being built. This means that there are no live versions, although there might be a website with basic program information, vision, white paper, etc.
- **Initial testing:** There might be a prototype or demo version of the tool, but it has not been widely disseminated and might not incorporate all elements.
- **Beta testing:** The tool has been fielded and is operational but is still in its beta phase, meaning that it is undergoing evaluation and assessment and might still have some bugs or limitations.
- **Fully operational:** The tool is fully operational and developed with all planned functionality.
- **Redevelopment:** The tool is being modified or updated for a new launch.
- **Unknown:** We used this term for cases in which we could not assess the level of development.

Intended Users

This field captures the names of the intended users of the tools. We have provided more than one in relevant cases. Knowing which audiences tools are aimed at allows users to seek out tools most relevant to their needs. Developers might also be interested in this information if it identifies underserved audiences, and funders might find this information useful if they hope to support the development of tools targeting specific types of individuals. The categories of intended users are

- the general public
- journalists
- researchers
- teachers and students.

Formal Evaluation

This field assesses whether a given tool has been formally evaluated. Formal evaluations typically require a randomized control trial (RCT) with pre/post testing. We found in our research that the vast majority of tools aimed at online disinformation have not been evaluated in any formal sense. Some tools report the broad results of internal reviews, and some discuss output metrics about their reach. For the purpose of this database, we consider not only RCTs but also a few other types of evaluations. First, we include those evaluations that compare performance across groups (users and non-users) and over time (before and after use). Second, we include evaluations of the tool performance; that is, whether the tool does what it says it does. This encompasses assessments of bot-detection tools that evaluate the tool's ability to identify bots and assessments of fact-checking tools on such criteria as objectivity and transparency. We note in the evaluation field what type of evaluations we identified for each tool. If we did not identify an evaluation, we noted "none found."

To summarize, in our search for evaluations:

- We looked for any formal evaluations of the tool that assessed its effect on targeted outcomes. This might be an assessment of the extent to which use of a fact-checking tool leads to updating of beliefs, or it might be an assessment of whether the implementation of codes and standards contributes to changes in user or journalist behavior.
- We considered evaluations assessing tool performance (that is, whether the tool did what it was supposed to), such as assessment

of the false positive rate of a bot detector or how often a media monitoring tool captures relevant pieces of disinformation. Similarly, fact-checking tools have been evaluated based on a set of best practices.

Link with Tech Platforms

We documented all known links between tool and web platforms, such as funding, partnerships, or having the tool integrated into a platform. Lack of information does not necessarily mean that there is no connection, however. We use "none found" to indicate that we did not find any such connections. Because platforms might be one of the primary targets of tools intended to counter disinformation, it is useful to understand when and where they could also be active in funding and developing these tools. From another perspective, having platforms that commit to incorporating or supporting certain tools after development could be a signal for funders because such support could contribute positively to the tool's success.

Summary

This chapter has described our approach to collecting information, the inclusion and exclusion criteria that determined which tools were captured in the database, and the dimensions (characteristics) that were provided for each tool. In the next chapter, we will provide descriptive statistics for these tools to provide insight into the numbers and types of disinformation tools available, their intended audiences, theories of change, and potential for achieving mass scale.

CHAPTER THREE

Descriptive Statistics

In this chapter, we use descriptive statistics to give interested users, researchers, and funders a high-level view of the 79 tools in the database. We provide types and numbers of resources available and the relationships between those resources, and we discuss common tool types, delivery methods, and theories of change. Because a tool could have more than one value for certain categories (e.g., tool type, delivery method) the total counts presented here might sum to a number greater than the total number of tools. However, if a tool has two delivery methods or does two things, we wanted to be able to capture both. We also consider cross-category comparison (for example, looking at the intersection of tool type and tool method or of tool type and tool cost) to understand more about the distribution of the tools and their interactions.

Tool Type

As a reminder, *tool type* refers to what the tool actually does—whether it verifies information, provides credibility-scoring, or detects bots. Our analysis of tool type takes into account each tool's primary and secondary tool types. Although most tools have only one type, some tools have more. In Table 3.1, when a tool has two different types, we count it twice, which is why the total is higher than the total number of tools in the database. As seen in Table 3.1, verification is the most common tool type, followed by education and training and then credibility-scoring. This distribution reflects the focus placed on identifying and correcting false information, as well as on media

Table 3.1
Tool Type Frequencies

Tool Type	Frequency
Bot and spam detection	3
Credibility-scoring	14
Codes and standards	5
Disinformation tracking	6
Verification	45
Whitelisting	5
Education and training	20
TOTAL	98

literacy and other educational activities as counters to the challenges of disinformation. Verification technologies are the most common, possibly because they target the most visible piece of the disinformation challenge—the disinformation itself—and have an information-focused theory of change that assumes that if we correct and remove false information, we can address the disinformation challenge.

However, verification tools also have disadvantages. First, they are typically applied *after* disinformation is already disseminated. Second, as described in more detail in Chapter Four, they might have limited effectiveness because of timing and individual user resistance. Education and training tools take a different, people-focused theory of change that tries to first improve users' skills and comprehension in ways that allow users to navigate the information system more effectively. Dual approaches—for example, an approach that uses both preventative measures available in education and training tools and reactive measures available in verification tools—might work well in countering disinformation. Evaluation would have to be undertaken to test this hypothesis. We describe each tool type in more detail in Chapter Four.

As noted, for the purpose of Table 3.1, we combine tool types 1 and 2. However, it is worth noting that only eight tools fell into more than one of our categories. Those tools with more than one type fell into several groups. About two thirds of these dual-type tools combined verification and credibility-scoring; bot and spam detection was combined with disinformation tracking. These tool type combinations show logical pairings for related or complementary tool functions. The verification and credibility-scoring pairing uses two methods intended to help consumers find reliable and accurate information. The latter pairing—bot and spam detection with disinformation tracking—combines two methods designed to uncover and identify untrustworthy information sources.

Method Used by Tool

Next, we look at the methods used by the tools (e.g., how each tool works). In Table 3.2, we show the breakdown by method used across 79 tools. The most common method used by disinformation tools in the database is machine learning and AI. About one-third of tools (n = 28) use some sort of automated method, whether an algorithm to identify bots and spam or some form of AI to detect when a photo or video's metadata have been manipulated. In Chapter Four, we discuss the types of AI used across different types of tools. That so many tools are relying on machine learning and AI is significant because using automated tools that operate without significant human input could be one way to develop a tool that can be scaled to take on the tremendous scope of the disinformation challenge.

Table 3.2
Frequency of Tool Methods

Method Type	Frequency
Machine learning and AI	28
Human implementation	21
Online course or game	19
Crowdsourcing	8
Blockchain	3
TOTAL	79

Human implementation is the second most common method ($n = 21$). It is the simplest method and one that can be implemented with few start-up costs, but it is also time-intensive and so might be harder to scale. The third most used method for disinformation tools is online courses and games ($n = 19$). Later, we will see that this method is used almost exclusively with one tool type: education and training. Other methods, such as the use of blockchain technology and crowdsourcing, are less frequent overall but common among some of the newer tools. Crowdsourcing, for example, is increasingly used as a means of verifying the accuracy of information and assessing source credibility. This method is less costly and time-consuming than human implementation methods but assumes that average users can accurately assess source credibility and information accuracy and that this accurate information will rise to the top.[1]

Delivery Platform

Next, we considered the possible delivery platforms in Table 3.3. Here, it is worth noting that many tools have more than one delivery platform. We consider total delivery platforms, summing across all delivery methods to understand the full set of ways that tools are accessible to users. The most common delivery platform is websites ($n = 55$), on which users can access information, input or upload photos for verification, or review

Table 3.3
Frequency of Delivery Methods

Delivery Platform	Frequency
App	4
Extension	19
Website	58
Other	2

---

[1]   For more on crowdsourcing, see Gordon Pennycook and David G. Rand, "Fighting Misinformation on Social Media Using Crowdsourced Judgments of News Source Quality," *PNAS*, Vol. 116, No. 7, 2019.

the source credibility rankings of different online or print news sources. Web extensions that can be downloaded and added to users' browsers were the next most common (n = 19); this approach is used most with credibility-scoring (almost one-half of credibility-scoring tools are delivered through extensions) and verification tools. Education and training tools are delivered almost exclusively through websites. Only a small percentage of tools are delivered through apps (n = 4), although the use of applications and mobile technologies might have the greatest potential for widespread scaling as people increasingly shift to mobile delivery and consumption of information. As tools mature, they could increasingly shift toward the development and use of applications for delivery of tools. This is a pattern we observed with tools in our database that did have an app version—they first developed in some other format (e.g., web extension), and then the app version followed. We have two tools with delivery platforms apart from the major ones listed here: One tool still is in development, and the other operates through an executable computer file.

Intended Users

Although we do not have data on how much the tools in the database are used, we do know from their marketing materials where they are aimed. Again, we consider all audiences here, so the total sums to greater than the total number of tools. The general public is clearly the primary audience of these tools, as seen in Table 3.4. Journalists are targeted less frequently then the general public but more frequently than researchers or teachers. This is not to say that these latter two groups do not have resources to turn to help them counter the effects of disinformation. Instead, they might rely on other products or platforms, their own research, scholarly journals, or more-traditional classroom training that, although valuable, do not qualify as tools. They also might use tools aimed at other audiences.[2]

---

[2] For more on media literacy education as a response to disinformation, see Alice Huguet, Jennifer Kavanagh, Garrett Baker, and Marjory S. Blumenthal, *Exploring Media Literacy Education as a Tool for Mitigating Truth Decay*, Santa Monica, Calif.: RAND Corporation, RR-3050-RC, 2019.

Table 3.4
Intended Users by Frequency

Intended Users	Frequency
General public	69
Journalists	19
Researchers	4
Teachers and students	8

Date of Origin

We also considered origin date, which is interesting from the perspective of understanding how the field has evolved and might continue to evolve. As shown in Figure 3.1, very few tools that we identified in our review originated between 1995 and 2014. It is possible that tools existed in non-online environments or that those tools that did exist have been updated and incorporated into new tools as the information ecosystem has evolved. After 2014, however, there was a sharp rise in online tools used to detect, counter, or defend against disinformation, peaking in 2017. It is possible that the visibility of disinformation during the leadup to the 2016 election inspired the rapid rise in tools the following year. In 2018, the number of new tools returned to near-2016 levels. It is unclear from these trends whether interest in developing disinformation tools is waning, the market for online tools is simply consolidating, or the slowing trend is driven by longer development times now that some of the low-hanging fruit has been plucked, leaving more-complex development challenges to tackle.

Funders

The tools identified in our review are supported by a variety of different funders. Almost all tools have more than one source of funding. It is worth noting that our analysis of funders relies on publicly available information. Some tools do not provide funding information, and even tools that do might not provide full details on all of their fund-

Figure 3.1
Number of Tools Originating by Year

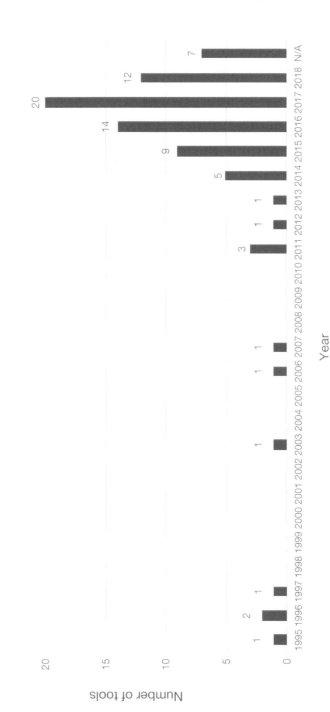

ing sources. It is nonetheless useful to understand the variety of different types of funding supporting civil society organizations and the tools they are developing to counter disinformation. *Civil society organizations,* the primary funders of tools, are foundations, institutes, initiatives, nongovernmental organizations, institutions of private education, and private donations. Some of the more-common civil society donors are the Knight Foundation and Craig Newmark Philanthropies. Some civil society funders are foundations of commercial entities. Commercial funders were the second most common type of funder. This category encompasses any for-profit entities and commercial (proprietary) funds received from the tool's own commercial efforts. Eight of the tools are funded, at least in part, by tech companies or their nonprofit arms. Examples of such funders are Facebook, The Facebook Journalism Project, Google, and the Google News Initiative. Government funders—funding from government organizations or publicly funded educational institutions—were the least common. There were also several funding sources that were unknown.

Maturity of Tools

We were also interested in understanding the level of development of tools in our database to understand the overall maturity of tools in the field and their development. Table 3.5 shows the distribution of tools by level of development and underscores that most tools in our data-

Table 3.5
Maturity Level of Tools

Maturity Level	Frequency
In development	9
Initial testing	1
Beta testing	3
Fully operational	65
In redevelopment	1

base are fully operational. It is worth noting that this likely reflects the fact that most tools are not heavily advertised until they are fully operational or well on their way to full development. As shown in Table 3.5, fewer than ten tools in the database are in development, and only a handful across types remain in beta or initial testing.

Method and Tool Type

In some cases, it is useful to consider multiple tool dimensions together. Figure 3.2, for example, shows how the identified tool methods are distributed across tool types. The most frequent tool type, verification, relies almost evenly on both machine learning and AI methods and on human implementation ones. There are few evaluations of these tools, or of whether the method that is used influences the effectiveness of the tool. The second most popular tool type, education and training, is almost exclusively delivered using an online course or game. In fact, online courses or games are only employed with education and training tools. The third most used tool, credibility-scoring, is almost evenly split between machine learning and AI methods and human imple-

Figure 3.2
Distribution of Methods Across Tool Types

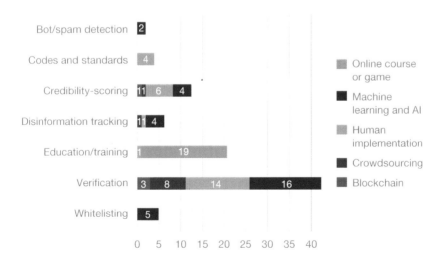

mentation ones, similar to verification. Finally, whitelisting tools are exclusively delivered using automated technologies. This makes sense because they work by screening out or capturing information coming from specific sites or individual senders. Crowdsourcing and blockchain methods are used largely with verification tools.

Tool Type and Intended User

Figure 3.3 compares tool type with intended audience (some tools were developed for two or more audiences, so these numbers will add up to more than the total 79 tools in the data set). Tools of all types are aimed at the general public. This is consistent with our observation that the majority of civil society tools identified in our review are aimed at the general public. Verification tools are the most common type of tool aimed at journalists. Only education and training tools are aimed at teachers and students explicitly, although as part of the general population, teachers and students might also use verification and other tools with broader audience aims. Tools aimed at researchers feature verification and disinformation tracking.

Figure 3.3
Tool Type by Intended Users

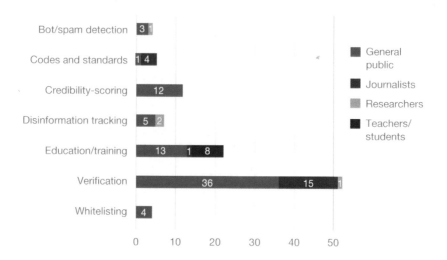

Qualitative Review of Theories Behind the Tools

Our final analysis considered the theory behind each tool. As noted already, *theory* refers to the discussion of how the tool works or its *theory of change*—i.e., how it works to counter disinformation. To analyze the theories of change, we reviewed theories for key themes and then categorized these themes into two primary categories: information-focused and people-focused. *Information-focused tools* are those that are designed with the belief that the key to addressing the disinformation challenge lies on the side of information provision and dissemination. Put another way, if higher-quality information is more readily available and if users are able to quickly find higher-quality information, this will serve as a counterweight to the threat posed by disinformation and those seeking to spread it. This better (or more accurate) information would be achieved either by identifying disinformation or upholding information standards through fact-checking, journalistic practices, or platform integrity. *People-focused tools* are based on the theory that affecting change in the person affects change in the consumption of information. This change would come through education, credibility-scoring, whitelists, bot detection, adjusting browser or platform settings, or increasing user awareness. Most of the people-focused tools use online courses or games as the method; most information-focused tools rely on machine learning and AI or human implementation. There are very few evaluations of these tools, which makes it difficult to assess the effectiveness of each of these two approaches or to make generalizations about which theory of change results in the best user outcomes. More-specific subthemes organized into broad themes used in categorizing the theory of change for each tool are as follows:

- information-focused
  - Identifying disinformation and low-quality sources allows users to consume better quality information.
  - Information standards can encourage production of higher-quality information.
- people-focused
  - Social engineering leads to habits that counter disinformation.

- Awareness of disinformation campaigns allows users to avoid and detect them.
- Awareness of different perspectives allows users to synthesize a more holistic interpretation of key issues and events.
- Media literacy education leads to better information choices.

Summary

This chapter provided an overview of the types of tools listed in the database. Several key themes emerged. First, verification tools are the most common, followed by education and training tools and credibility-scoring. Second, the most common method behind the tools in the database continues to be machine learning and AI. Third, most tools are still delivered via websites rather than via mobile applications, even though the latter are likely to be more widely used and more versatile. Most tools are fully operational and focus on content over process. Finally, tools most often adopted an information-focused theory of change aimed at improving the quality of information as a means to tackle the disinformation challenge, but there are also a large number of tools aimed at improving user skills and reducing individual susceptibility to disinformation.

We lack good evaluative research to assess the effects of these different tools. This prevents us from assessing whether certain tool types or delivery platforms are more effective at reaching audiences or addressing the disinformation challenge. In the next chapter, we will discuss in more detail what we know about how each major tool type works and evidence that exists about which tools work more or less effectively than others.

CHAPTER FOUR

Deep Dives: Tool Types

This chapter provides a deeper dive on each of the seven tool types in the database. We provide information on the pros and cons of each type of tool and whether a given tool type is likely to work and why. We also describe evaluations and discuss examples, offering insight into the range of different variations, even within each tool type category.

Bot and Spam Detection

One common type of counter-disinformation tool involves detecting automated accounts, such as bots or spam. From a technical perspective, a bot is a few lines of code executing tasks on an online website. A *bot* could be written for a social media site, such as Twitter, and carries out messaging or retweeting tasks faster than a human could. Bots have been able to take over online conversations with disinformation that is easily retweeted by unsuspecting users. Bots have also been identified as targeting specific users to influence or harass them to advance a political, social, or other motive. *Spam*, on the other hand, is unwanted information, usually in high volume, sent to an online account. Spammers can be particularly effective in spreading misinformation through the use of automated accounts.[1]

Large social media platforms, such as Twitter and Facebook, have been independently proactive about identifying and removing bots and

---

[1] Eni Mustafaraj and Panagiotis Metaxas, "The Fake News Spreading Plague: Was It Preventable?" *Proceedings of the ACM Web Science*, Troy, N.Y., 2017.

other automated accounts, especially those known to be linked with foreign entities. However, bots and automated accounts have so deeply permeated social media platforms that they are unlikely to be fully eliminated. Third-party organizations have also taken on a role in this area, becoming more active in bot detection. Here, we consider how these organizations might supplement efforts by technology and social media companies. There are many challenges associated with detecting bots—not only are there far too many for any one program or actor to identify, but bot programmers also adapt quickly to evade detection. Third-party organizations will never have the ability to remove content from a social media platform. But by flagging bots, these organizations might be able to address a piece of the challenge. Bot-detecting tools do have an important limitation, however: They operate almost exclusively on Twitter, which limits their reach in tackling online disinformation.

Tools that can identify bots (and other types of automated accounts) provide greater transparency about sources of information. Individuals might judge the credibility and trustworthiness of information provided by bots differently than information that comes from a person. In this way, bot detection can help individuals make decisions about what information to trust.

The best-known bot detector is called Botometer—a collaboration between the Indiana University Network Science Institute (IUNI) and the Center for Complex Networks and Systems Research (CNetS)—which assesses a Twitter account's recent activity (shares, followers, followed accounts, tweets, etc.) and uses machine learning and algorithms (trained on thousands of decisions made by human coders) to determine the likelihood that the original account is a bot.[2] Botometer gives each account a score between 0 and 1, with a higher score indicating a higher likelihood that the account is a bot.[3]

---

[2] Botometer, homepage, undated; Stefan Wojcik, Solomon Messing, Aaron Smith, Lee Rainie, and Paul Hitlin, "Bots in the Twittersphere," Pew Research Center, April 9, 2018.

[3] Onur Varol, Emilio Ferrara, Clayton A. Davis, Filippo Menczer, and Alessandro Flammini, "Online Human-Bot Interactions: Detection, Estimation, and Characterization," *Proceedings of the Eleventh International AAAI Conference on Web and Social Media*, 2017, p. 282.

Since the release of our original database (to which the data in Chapter Three is related), we have continued to add new tools—including more-sophisticated bot-detection tools, such as BotSlayer, which "uses an anomaly-detection algorithm to flag hashtags, links, accounts, and media that are trending and amplified in a coordinated fashion by likely bots. A Web dashboard lets users explore the tweets and accounts associated with suspicious campaigns via Twitter, visualize their spread via Hoaxy, and search related images and content on Google."[4] The purpose of BotSlayer is to make real-time monitoring of misinformation campaigns easier.[5]

The creators of Botometer and BotSlayer have cautioned that "[a] supervised machine learning tool is only as good as the data used for its training. Social bots evolve rapidly, and even the most advanced algorithms will fail with outdated training datasets."[6] They explain that classification models will have to be updated using new data and new user feedback. The features that are used to distinguish "between human behaviors and increasingly complex bot behaviors" will also have to be updated as bots become more sophisticated.[7] This underscores just how dynamic bots and the disinformation ecosystem can be and emphasizes the significant challenge faced by those trying to counter it.

Botometer and BotSlayer both have open source technology, which means that they can be updated and improved more easily and that other technologies can be built on top of them. For example, Botson is a Chrome plugin that blurs the tweets sent by accounts with a high bot score from Botometer and instead provides information about these accounts.[8] Another tool built off Botometer is actually a bot itself, a

---

[4] BotSlayer, homepage, undated.

[5] Kevin Fryling, "How to Slay a Bot," *Science Node*, September 22, 2019.

[6] Kai-Cheng Yang, Onur Varol, Clayton A. Davis, Emilio Ferrara, Alessandro Flammini, and Filippo Menczer, "Arming the Public with Artificial Intelligence to Counter Social Bots," *Human Behavior & Emerging Technology*, Vol. 1, No. 1, 2019, p. 55.

[7] Yang et al., 2019, p. 55.

[8] Josh Constine, "Disrupt Hackathon App Notim.Press/Ed Algorithmically Detects Fake News," *TechCrunch*, December 4, 2016.

Twitter account known as @probabot, which searches Twitter to identify bots using the Botometer scores. There are other bot-detecting
tools, such as Botcheck.me, which is the brainchild of a tech startup
working toward creating a "safer internet,"[9] and private companies that
offer bot-detection and blocking services (e.g., ShieldSquare).[10]

Bot-detection tools can help Twitter users make better choices
about what types of information to consume. However, the ability of
bots to counter disinformation is user-dependent—and, again, limited
largely to Twitter. Furthermore, once individuals know that a given
account is run by bots, there is no guarantee that they will choose to
disregard or distrust the information provided by that bot.

Credibility-Scoring

Another set of tools comprises those focused on evaluating the overall
credibility of a website, a source, or an article. This is different from
fact-checking or verification. To make the distinction clear, individual
pieces of information can be fact-checked, but a newspaper might be
given a low credibility score. Credibility-scoring initiatives also vary in
their format (e.g., browser extension, website, or app) and the details of
how they work.[11]

One tool that uses credibility-scoring is FakerFact. FakerFact has
trained a machine-learning algorithm, Walt, on several types of factual
and less factual styles of writing, such as journalism articles, scientific
journal articles, satire, narrative fiction, op-eds, blogs, politically biased

---

[9] In addition to Botcheck (the startup), RoBhat Labs has a project called SurfSafe, discussed in the verification section. See RoBhat Labs, homepage, undated. Although not tech-
nically a nonprofit, RoBhat Labs has an explicit mission aimed at benefiting society and is
not working on any for-profit tools, so we include it.

[10] Botcheck.me, "Detect & Track Twitter Bots," webpage, undated; Radware, "Stop Bots in
Real-Time with ShieldSquare Anti-Bot Solution," webpage, 2019.

[11] One of the best examples of a credibility-scoring tool is NewsGuard, which assigns
reliability ratings to news sources. They offer a free browser extension for users, as well as
licenses for advertisers and internet and mobile providers. Because it's a for-profit company,
however, it is outside the purview of this report. NewsGuard, homepage, undated.

news, and hate speech. FakerFact does not provide truth or falsehood ratings. It leaves that judgment up to the user. Instead, it provides ratings for characteristics of the article, such as whether the article is journalistic, sensational, agenda-driven, wiki, opinion, or satire. Users can upload an article to Walt, which will classify the purpose and objectivity of the article, and users can then decide how much they trust or believe the article.[12] Users also can install the browser extension, after which they can click the icon while viewing any article, which will produce a score.[13]

Trusted Times is another credibility-scoring platform that relies only on machine learning to classify bias. It rates the source as fake, unreliable, verified, or mainstream, and offers an analysis of the article, by extracting all of the relevant subjects and determining whether the tone is positive, negative, or neutral. Trusted Times also provides a pattern analysis of the author's previous coverage and a pattern analysis of the source over time.[14]

Credibility-scoring could be a powerful tool in combating disinformation. It allows users to judge how much to trust a news site and might prompt them to move to other news sources shown to be more trustworthy. However, we were not able to find any empirical assessments evaluating the extent to which these tools are able to change user behavior or to improve the accuracy of news consumed by users.

Codes and Standards

Codes and standards aim to set quality benchmarks for news producers, and in some cases, news consumers. There are several types of codes and standards, but they all share the creation of a set of principles or processes that they ask members to commit and adhere to in return for some outward sign of membership that can be recognized by others. Some codes and standards focus on news producers, setting standards

---

[12] FakerFact, "About FakerFact," webpage, undated-a.

[13] FakerFact, "How to Use Fakerfact," webpage, undated-b.

[14] Trusted Times, "How to Use Trusted Times," webpage, undated.

for journalists or news outlets or organizations; others target news consumers with a set of desired behaviors. These tools do not score news
sources for accuracy or quality the way a credibility-scoring tool does,
and they do not verify or fact-check information the way verification
tools do. Instead, these tools create standards that deal with processes
and behaviors for information production and consumption, ask companies and/or individuals to commit to this standard or code, and then
certify their participation (but do not always verify their adherence).
Tools vary in the extent to which they have mechanisms to hold members accountable for the commitments made and the types of monitoring conducted. In many cases, the individual or the organization is
responsible for self-policing. We consider these a tool for the purpose of
this report because people are able to interact with them in an abstract
sense and because they are a key innovation advocated by civil society
organizations to counter online disinformation.

A variety of news organizations and nonprofits have been involved
in developing codes and standards that are listed in our database. As an
example, the Trust Project is a collaboration among several news companies to set journalistic standards called Trust Indicators, featuring
such factors as author expertise, citations and references, diverse voices,
and actionable feedback.[15] When news sources meet the standards set
by the Trust Project, a "Trust Mark" is included on those sources' pages
as a signal to users of having met the required standard. This standard was developed by Santa Clara University's Markkula Center for
Applied Ethics and is now independent.[16] The Trust Project partners
with news, social media, and search engine companies to display and
use these Trust Indicators for news sites that merit them. These indicators were informed by interviews in which news consumers were asked
when and why they trust news. After these interviews, a collaboration
of 100 news companies, including *The Economist*, the *Washington Post*,
and the *Globe and Mail*, developed the Trust Indicators. The indicators
certify that the news outlets receiving them publish trustworthy news.

---

[15] Trust Project, "Frequently Asked Questions," webpage, undated.

[16] Anne Eigeman, "Trust Project Goes Independent to Help Public Distinguish News from
Nonsense," *Nonprofit Quarterly*, June 4, 2019.

The Trust Project also features disclosures about the news company's standards for ethics, fairness, and accuracy, the organization's agenda, the journalist's background and expertise, and the work that went into reporting the news story.

Such companies as Facebook have started using the Trust Indicators in multiple ways, as have search engines, such as Google and Bing. They display the Trust Indicators themselves, and also integrate the indicators into their algorithms. For example, the Trust Project says, "Facebook uses the Best Practices Trust Indicator in its process to index news pages, and Bing uses Trust Indicator labels to display whether an article is news, opinion or analysis, providing information that people need to understand an article's context."[17] Other tools for countering misinformation, such as NewsGuard, also use the Trust Indicators. Many partners also display the Trust Project's Trust Mark on their sites.[18]

Researchers at the Center for Media Engagement at the University of Texas–Austin, with support from the Trust Project, conducted an experiment about the effects of various types of Trust Indicators. The 1,183 American adults in the study read an online news article that contained either Trust Indicators or no Trust Indicators.[19] The researchers found small but statistically significant effects of the Trust Indicators on the perceptions of news consumers. Readers found the articles with indicators to be more trusted and more reputable. Those who read articles with indicators "also had a stronger sense that the news outlet told the whole story and was more reliable than those who read articles without indicators."[20]

---

[17] Trust Project, undated.

[18] Trust Project, undated.

[19] The Trust Indicators used were (1) information about the reporter; (2) a label indicating that the article was "analysis" (as opposed to "opinion," "news," "review," or "advertiser content"), with a link to Trust Project–defined article types; (3) footnotes with source material; (4) a "Behind the Story" section with sources and best practices; and (5) information about the news organization's participation in the Trust Project. Alex Curry and Natalie Jomini Stroud, *Trust in Online News*, University of Texas at Austin, Center for Media Engagement, December 12, 2017, p. 1.

[20] Curry and Stroud, 2017, pp. 2–3.

The Pro-Truth Pledge uses a different mechanism; instead of holding journalists and companies accountable to codes and standards, it holds media consumers accountable. The Pro-Truth Pledge asks media consumers and public figures to apply codes and standards to how they consume news and allows individuals to hold themselves responsible. The Pledge uses strategies informed by behavioral science to increase sharing, honoring, and encouraging truthful media, especially among politicians. It encourages politicians to commit to truthful communications by creating a groundswell of others who have also made the Pro-Truth Pledge and then calling on their representatives to do the same.[21] The Pledge commits a person to 12 behaviors that help them share truthful media (such as by fact-checking and citing their posts and sharing the whole truth, even when some of it negates the person's opinion), honor truth (by reevaluating and retracting information when one cannot verify it and aligning opinions and actions with true information), and encourage truth (by compassionately educating others in using reliable sources and celebrating those who retract statements or update beliefs based on falsehoods).[22] This particular code or standard aims to fight disinformation by increasing the amount of quality information available, increasing organizational and consumer commitment to quality information, and encouraging information users to seek out higher quality information. According to one underpowered ($n = 21$) study, researchers affiliated with the Pro-Truth Pledge found that Facebook users posted more-truthful posts four weeks after taking the pledge.[23] However, the use of codes and standards (and other rating methods, such as the credibility-scoring discussed previously) have led to some unintended consequences, such as users displaying the opposite of the intended behavior by clicking on untrusted sources more frequently. Furthermore, without true accountability

---

[21] Gleb Tsipursky, "The Pro-Truth Pledge: An Effective Strategy for Skeptics to Fight Fake News and Post-Truth Politics," *Skeptic*, undated.

[22] Pro-Truth Pledge, homepage, undated.

[23] Gleb Tsipursky, Fabio Votta, and Kathryn M. Roose, "Fighting Fake News and Post-Truth Politics with Behavioral Science: The Pro-Truth Pledge," *Behavior and Social Issues*, Vol. 27, 2018, p. 64.

mechanisms (such as monitoring and enforcement), it is not clear that codes and standards really change the behavior of users or even the habits of journalists overall and over the longer term.

Disinformation Tracking

Rather than score a news source's credibility or rate its compliance with different codes and standards, a disinformation tracker literally tracks disinformation: These tools either trace specific pieces of disinformation and their spread over time or assess the level of fake or misleading news on a particular platform. These tools predominantly use machine learning and AI, with some functions accomplished through crowdsourcing in the form of users reporting ads. The aims of these tools are to increase awareness of disinformation campaigns and online ad targeting and to draw attention to and offer insights on how information spreads online.

For example, the University of Michigan's Center for Social Media Responsibility has created what they call "the Iffy Quotient" to track how often misleading stories are shared on Facebook and Twitter.[24] The Iffy Quotient aims to create a version of a credit rating for global news sources, based on the likelihood that a given source carries disinformation. The tracker uses two other disinformation tracking sites to produce and publish its quotient. It first links with NewsWhip, which tracks the creation of new URLs from more than 400,000 sites daily. NewsWhip also reports how engaging each story was for users on Facebook and Twitter (i.e., how many likes, shares, retweets, and other interactions each story received on each platform). The Iffy Quotient takes the top 5,000 most-engaging URLs from that day, strips them to their domain name, and uses Media Bias/Fact Check (a credibility-scoring and fact-checking website) to classify the domain names of each URL as Iffy, OK, or Unknown. The percentage of Iffy sources compared with the whole is the Iffy Quotient for that platform on that

---

[24] Jacqueline Thomsen, "Researchers Unveil Tool to Track Disinformation on Social Media," *The Hill*, October 10, 2018.

day. From January to November 2016, the Iffy Quotient on both Facebook and Twitter nearly doubled. Facebook has since returned to early 2016 levels; Twitter has not declined.[25] The tracker's creators hope the Iffy Quotient will act as an "external benchmark of veracity to reassure readers and advertisers," hold social media companies responsible for progress in countering disinformation, and verify the progress that companies make.[26] The Iffy Quotient has been relied on by prominent researchers in the field as a tool with which to track disinformation,[27] but there has not been research about the effectiveness of the tool itself.

Another disinformation tracker is the Hamilton 2.0 (initially known as Hamilton 68) dashboard, which was created by the newly formed Alliance for Securing Democracy, which tracks Russian disinformation and propaganda efforts on Twitter. The first version, Hamilton 68, tracked 600 accounts with clear connections to Russia. The accounts included bots and real users. The accounts were tracked in real time, and the categories of data produced were hashtags, topics (terms used), and links. Each category was analyzed according to top items (most tweeted in prior 48 hours) and trending items (highest percent increase in prior 48 hours).[28] The new dashboard, Hamilton 2.0, which launched in September 2019, tracks only about 150 Twitter accounts in two categories: "those of the Russian government and diplomatic corps and those connected to Russian state-funded media."[29] Unlike Hamilton 68, it publishes a full list of all the accounts it tracks, and it does not track bots.[30] Specifically, Hamilton 2.0 provides analysis of topics and stories shared and boosted

---

[25] Laurel Thomas, "U-M Tool Measures 'Iffy' News on Social Media in Time for 2018 Election," *Michigan News*, University of Michigan, October 10, 2018.

[26] Clare Melford, Alexandra Mousavizadeh, and Danny Rogers, "A Global Disinformation Index—A Step in the Right Direction," *Medium*, April 12, 2018.

[27] For example, see Allcott, Gentzkow, and Yu, 2019.

[28] J. M. Berger, "The Methodology of the Hamilton 68 Dashboard," Alliance for Securing Democracy, August 7, 2017.

[29] Bret Schafer, "Hamilton 2.0 Methodology and FAQs," Alliance for Securing Democracy, September 3, 2019.

[30] Schafer, 2019.

on Twitter, television, and news websites by Russian government and state-backed media sources.

As a final example, Hoaxy is a media monitoring tool developed by Indiana University that tracks the spread of disinformation articles online and visualizes this spread across time. Hoaxy searches for both unverified claims and fact-checked claims going back to 2016. It tracks links shared from both low-credibility sources and independent fact-checking organizations and visualizes the spread of information and disinformation. Hoaxy's interactive visualizations show how these articles spread from user to user, and visualizations can be paused and viewed more closely at any time index. Hoaxy also calculates a *bot score* for each node or user, which is a measure of the likely level of automation of an account. It also allows users to conduct their own searches for disinformation articles on Twitter for the past seven days. The tool raises awareness of the spread of disinformation online and offers insights regarding how specific articles spread online.[31] Once again, however, we have not been able to locate formal evaluations documenting how disinformation tracking tools influence user behaviors.

Verification

Verification tools make up the largest group of counter-disinformation tools, by far. This group consists of tools that check facts and those that verify the authenticity of images or videos. Private organizations, non-profits, and universities are all active in the area of fact-checking, providing third-party verification of information and images and developing both reference websites and automated online tools that allow users to fact-check information or verify the authenticity of photos and videos. Fact-checking can serve many purposes in the fight against disinformation. It can identify and correct information that is inaccurate, and it can help readers gauge the credibility of different pieces of information. Of course, fact-checking on its own is not likely to solve the disinformation problem. Malicious actors can spread false information more quickly

---

[31] Hoaxy, "FAQ Index," webpage, undated.

than fact-checkers can verify and correct it, and although some individuals will update their beliefs in response to new data, many will hold firm to their initial perceptions. Research on how willing people are to update their beliefs and under what circumstances they will change their minds is somewhat mixed. Authors of a meta-analysis from 2019 attempted to bring clarity to this question of when, where, and how fact-checking works. The authors reviewed 30 studies from 20 research reports.[32] They found that the effect of fact-checking on beliefs was both positive and significant.[33] As predicted by the authors, and common sense, fact-checking that debunked opposing ideology had a stronger effect than did fact-checking that debunked one's own ideology. The analysis revealed no significant differences in the effects of fact-checking on people who self-identified as Democrats or liberals versus Republicans or conservatives but did indicate that fact-checking was less effective on individuals who are more politically engaged, perhaps because these individuals are more set in their beliefs.[34] It also identified interesting differences in the ways that fact-checking affected Democrats versus Republicans. The effect of ideology-debunking and ideology-confirming fact-checking on Democrats was the same, whereas for Republicans the effect of confirmatory fact-checks was much greater.[35] The authors of this analysis also found that inclusion of visual aids and graphics weakened the effect of the fact-check, and that the length of the fact-check report had no effect. More-complex language, however, did weaken effectiveness. The authors found that fact-checking articles that featured rating scales were most effective, followed by articles without scales, and that fact-checking labels were least effective.[36]

In the summary of their findings, the authors explained that although fact-checking can have positive effects, there are major weak-

---

[32] Nathan Walter, Jonathan Cohen, R. Lance Holbert, and Yasmin Morag, "Fact-Checking: A Meta-Analysis of What Works and for Whom," *Political Communication*, 2019, p. 8.

[33] Walter et al., 2019, p. 11.

[34] Walter et al., 2019, p. 12.

[35] Walter et al., 2019, p. 15.

[36] Walter et al., 2019, pp. 15–16.

nesses. Most notably, even if fact-checking can have moderate effects on correcting specific beliefs, a larger question is whether this practice can change worldviews or help users become better at identifying the tell-tale signs of disinformation campaigns.

There are many ongoing efforts in the area of third-party fact-checking. The most-basic fact-checking efforts rely on human assessment and research, publishing detailed "fact-checks" about key issues, questions, debates, and conspiracies. Politifact, for example, conducts detailed analyses of the statements of leading political figures and assesses their accuracy on a scale from "true" to "pants on fire." Politifact relies on many sources to build a comprehensive fact-check of a false claim, usually relying on other fact-checking efforts, searches of Google and online databases, expert consultations, a review of various publications, and a final review of all available evidence.[37]

Politifact has been criticized for being partisan in the sources it uses and its approach to debunking facts.[38] However, Media Bias/Fact Check has assessed Politifact as "least biased," its highest available rating.[39] Snopes.com and Factcheck.org provide types of information that are similar to Politifact, identifying and debunking conspiracy theories, analyzing claims, and evaluating evidence.[40] These tools are typically web-based, with a website providing a central location for relevant fact-checked information. Other tools are similar. The "Share the Facts" widget, developed at Duke University, similarly relies on humans to conduct fact-checks and then provides fact-checked claims and other information both in the form of an app and on a website.[41]

A related approach to fact-checking and verification focuses more on creating a single source with as much available factual information

---

[37] Angie Drobnic Holan, "The Principles of the Truth-O-Meter: PolitiFact's Methodology for Independent Fact-Checking," *Politifact*, February 12, 2018.

[38] Eric Ostermeier, "Selection Bias? PolitiFact Rates Republican Statements as False at 3 Times the Rate of Democrats," *Smart Politics*, February 10, 2011.

[39] Media Bias/Fact Check, "Politifact," webpage, August 12, 2018.

[40] Snopes, "About Us," webpage, undated; FactCheck.org, "Our Process," webpage, May 3, 2019.

[41] Share the Facts, "About," webpage, undated.

as possible. One example is USAFacts, run by Steve Ballmer,[42] which is dedicated to the collection and curation of federal, state, and local government data and information for free public use.[43] If such repositories could gain the public trust and maintain credibility, they would be a valuable resource.

Because human fact-checking is time-intensive and costly, there are many ongoing efforts to develop automated or crowdsourced platforms able to verify information with minimal human involvement. Most of these efforts have been developed by for-profit companies, with the exception of Bitpress. The founders describe the venture as a "blockchain-based ledger of trust that leverages a decentralized network of journalists to determine the credibility of news."[44] Bitpress uses a "data science platform" to identify which stories to fact-check. It selects those with a high impact score (which calculates how widely the article has been read or shared on various social media platforms) that have been contradicted by various news sources. Human fact-checkers then verify the story and provide a misinformation alert that lists a rating (true, probably true, uncertain, probably false, false, misleading, or opinion) and other relevant information, such as the reason behind the rating.[45] Bitpress assigns each false claim a fingerprint (or a unique identifier) so that it can be identified in its various forms and provides the fingerprint to platforms and consumers.[46]

Other organizations provide verification tools and strategies focused on specific types of information—the accuracy or credibility of photos or videos, for example. First Draft, part of Harvard's Shorenstein Center, has produced a one-hour, online course that trains users in verifying information, such as the location and date of photos and the accuracy of reporting. It also provides a verification toolbox with

---

[42] USAFacts, homepage, undated-b.

[43] USAFacts, "About Us," webpage, undated-a.

[44] Lloyd Armbrust, Eric Oetker, Jonathan Dawe, April Halasz, and Zach Beasley, *Bitpress: News on the Blockchain*, Bitpress, March 10, 2018.

[45] Bitpress, "Our Process," webpage, undated-b.

[46] Bitpress, "The Fingerprint for Misinformation," webpage, undated-a.

a variety of tools that can assist in the verification and fact-checking process, such as a reverse image search, weather checks to verify date and time, and ways to link individual names with Twitter usernames and Facebook profiles.[47] There is also a nontrivial number of image verification tools. The Frame by Frame plugin for YouTube videos can assist users seeking to verify video clips by allowing them to view clips one frame at a time to identify oddities that might indicate that a video had been manipulated or faked.[48]

The tech startup RoBhat Labs has a tool called SurfSafe, a plug-in that allows users to instantly verify where a photo they're viewing has been posted before, and surfaces the first known appearance of the photo. It also gives users the option of labeling the photo as propaganda, misleading, or Photoshopped, to help further refine the Surf-Safe model.[49]

Amnesty International's Citizen Evidence Lab, directed at human rights workers and researchers, offers various tools and methods for verifying "user-generated content for human rights defense."[50] One such tool is the YouTube Data Viewer, which allows users to extract the exact upload time and all thumbnails from videos.[51] This tool is useful beyond human rights work, and was cited by journalist Craig Silverman, a 'fake news' expert, as one of "the core, free verification tools in the verification toolkit."[52] In a related effort, Silverman developed a

---

[47] First Draft, "Verification Toolbox," webpage, undated-b: First Draft, "Education Area," webpage, undated-a.

[48] Alastair Reid, "7 Vital Browser Plugins for Newsgathering and Verification," First Draft, August 26, 2016.

[49] Issie Lapowsky, "This Browser Extension Is Like an Antivirus for Fake Photos," *Wired*, August 20, 2018.

[50] Citizen Evidence Lab, "About & FAQ," webpage, undated.

[51] Citizen Evidence Lab, "YouTube Data Viewer," webpage, July 1, 2014.

[52] Craig Silverman, "Amnesty International Launches Video Verification Tool, Website," Poynter, July 8, 2014.

verification handbook to aid information consumers in verifying digital information during crisis situations, such as after a major disaster.[53]

These fact-checking and verification tools are clearly a part of the solution to the disinformation problem. On their own, however, they are unlikely to solve the problem because of several challenges. First, the amount of disinformation far exceeds the capacity of fact-checking tools. Second, fact-checking tools typically require an engaged user who is interested in identifying what is factual and what is not. Research on cognitive biases reminds us that individuals often reject information that does not confirm their beliefs and are often unwilling to seek out information that could undermine or contradict those beliefs.[54] Individuals might be hesitant or uninterested in using fact-checking tools—and, even when they do use them, they might reject the information provided, limiting the possible utility of such tools. If some of these tools were automatically provided to users through partnerships with social media platforms, that might have a more substantive effect. Third, fact-checking tools are not perfect, especially when driven by algorithms and AI. They might misidentify false information as true or trustworthy or label true information or websites as false. Efforts to improve and increase the role that fact-checking plays in fighting the spread of disinformation should focus on improving the quality and efficiency of automated fact-checking tools. As these tools become more advanced and sophisticated, their accuracy might improve, but they are still likely to have a non-negligible failure rate. Finally, there are so many different fact-checking options that even interested users might be perplexed about which tools to use. From this perspective, there might be advantages to funneling research toward understanding which tools work most effectively and

---

[53] Verification Handbook, homepage, undated; Brendan Nyhan and Jason Reifler, "When Corrections Fail: The Persistence of Political Misperceptions," *Political Behavior*, Vol. 32, No. 2, June 2010.

[54] Brendan Nyhan and Jason Reifler, *Misinformation and Fact-Checking: Research Findings from Social Science*, Media Policy Institute, February 2012; Daniel Kahneman and Shane Frederick, "Representativeness Revisited: Attribute Substitution in Intuitive Judgment," in Thomas Gilovich, Dale Griffin, and Daniel Kahneman, eds., *Heuristics and Biases: The Psychology of Intuitive Judgment*, Cambridge: Cambridge University Press, 2002.

improving those that show the most promise both in terms of accurately identifying false information and in terms of user uptake.

Whitelisting

Whitelists are another type of information-focused tool that could be used in combating disinformation. A blacklist keeps undesirable sources out; a whitelist allows desirable sources in. Common in the computer security arena because of the evolving nature of malware, "whitelisting limits use with a 'deny by default' approach so that only approved files or applications can be installed."[55] This concept has been adopted more recently by people interested in combating fake news. The idea is that either institutions or brands create whitelists of acceptable or reliable content or sources.[56] In the corporate world, whitelists already exist. For example, JPMorgan Chase began using a whitelist for its advertising strategy after it discovered an ad for its services on a fake news website called "Hillary 4 Prison."[57] In the United Kingdom, Vodafone worked with Google, Facebook, and advertising agencies to create a list of acceptable sites on which it would run ads. Vodafone explained that although "it is relatively easy to blacklist certain sites, such as those relating to porn and gambling . . . it is difficult to exclude content that is—in editorial terms—at odds with an advertiser's own principles and beliefs."[58] A whitelist, created using human judgment, was the best way to "ensure brand safety" so that only those whitelisted

---

[55] Drew Robb, "Whitelisting: Why and How It Works," *eSecurity Planet*, September 24, 2014.

[56] Sandra Baron and Rebecca Crootof, *Fighting Fake News: Workshop Report*, New Haven, Conn.: Information Society Project, The Floyd Abrams Institute for Freedom of Expression, Yale Law School, undated.

[57] Sapna Maheshwari, "Chase Had Ads on 400,000 Sites. Then on Just 5,000. Same Results," *New York Times*, March 29, 2017.

[58] Mark Sweney, "Vodafone to Stop Its Ads Appearing on Fake News and Hate Speech Sites," *The Guardian*, June 6, 2017.

sites could receive Vodafone's advertising revenue.[59] Whitelisting is also gaining popularity with other corporations that are conscious of which companies they support with their advertising funds.

Whitelists are being created in other ways to better serve the needs of individual users. Browser extensions or applications allow users to whitelist websites that their computer is allowed to visit. Website Whitelist is one such tool, which allows access only to sites on user-approved whitelists. In addition, it also automatically blocks external tracking and advertising sites.[60]

Another tool, Adblock Plus, uses machine learning and AI to automatically whitelist ads rather than websites. If ads meet the "acceptable ads" standards, those ads are allowed through. A user can also manually set what types of ads are displayed.[61] These tools also block cookies and trackers that monitor individual browsing, thereby reducing microtargeting, which allows more-sophisticated disinformation vehicles to find targets among news consumers.

Education and Training

Taking a different approach from tracking disinformation and rating news sources, this set of counter-disinformation tools focuses on news consumers and fortifying them against disinformation, primarily through media literacy. The field of media literacy education is too vast to cover in much detail here. However, a treatment of how third-party organizations are contributing to the fight against disinformation would be incomplete without a short discussion of the role they play in developing media literacy curricula and programming. Previous RAND research covers media literacy education tools, curricula, activities, and other programs.[62]

---

[59] Sweney, 2017.

[60] Website Whitelist, version 6.2.3, May 12, 2018.

[61] Adblock Plus, version 3.7, October 22, 2019.

[62] Huguet et al., 2019.

Third-party organizations have been very active in the media literacy field, with a particular focus on students from kindergarten through high school and, to a lesser extent, in college and university settings. Media literacy programming varies in duration and format, ranging from short online modules to full academic courses that mix in-person instruction with online coursework. Many newer media literacy interventions have focused primarily on news literacy and on how to navigate digital and social media, but others explore advertising, entertainment media, cybersecurity and privacy, and civic engagement. They teach students a variety of different skills—critical thinking; the ability to evaluate news sources; and the ability to search for and find information, identify biases, and navigate digital spaces (including sharing information). There are many organizations active in this space: universities, such as the Media Education Lab at the University of Rhode Island; for-profit companies, such as the Center for Media Literacy and other, smaller education-oriented firms; and nonprofits, such as the News Literacy Project, run by journalist Alan Miller. In our database, we focus on a particular type of media literacy programming: online games and activities aimed at advancing media literacy among tool users. We exclude curricula that are more static in nature because of our assessment that these are not, in fact, tools.

In theory, media literacy education, including online games and activities, holds promise as a tool against disinformation. If individuals are better able to separate fact from opinions or fiction, to assess the credibility of sources, to identify disinformation, and to search for and find facts when they need them, they might be less susceptible to disinformation campaigns and more likely to use fact-checking and bot-detection technologies. The question is, do these programs work? To date, we do not have the information needed to make a complete assessment. Few of the programs described here, and few of the programs we were able to identify, have been rigorously and formally evaluated (or at least have evaluations that have been made public) to determine whether they affect student outcomes. In fact, there is not even consensus on what student outcome metrics should be used to assess the effectiveness of these programs.

The evaluations that have occurred have shown some promising results. For example, a study of a curriculum known as *Beyond Blame: Challenging Violence in the Media* showed that students who completed the program were more likely to see a connection between violence in the media and an individual's appetite for violence. Only those students who received the program from teachers trained to provide the course, however, saw an improvement in their media literacy skills.[63]

Another study focused on the effect of any media literacy training rather than evaluating any particular program. In an online nationally representative survey of youths aged 15 to 27, participants were asked questions about a series of simulated posts that varied with respect to ideological position and type of argument used.[64] They were also asked how often they had "[d]iscussed how to tell if the information you find online is trustworthy" and "[d]iscussed the importance of evaluating the evidence that backs up people's opinions" in class.[65] The researchers found that respondents "who reported having media literacy learning opportunities were no more likely than others to be influenced by directional motivation but were significantly more likely to be influenced by accuracy motivation."[66] *Directional motivation* is defined as the desire to justify a conclusion that matches your existing beliefs, whereas *accuracy motivation* is guided by the desire to process information carefully and using complex rules.[67] The study's authors noted that this demonstrates the importance of media literacy education, but that a shortcoming of their study was its reliance on self-reports. They

---

[63] Theresa Webb and Kathryn Martin, "Evaluation of a US School-Based Media Literacy Violence Prevention Curriculum on Changes in Knowledge and Critical Thinking Among Adolescents," *Journal of Children and Media*, Vol. 6, No. 4, 2012.

[64] Joseph Kahne and Benjamin Bowyer, "Educating for Democracy in a Partisan Age: Confronting the Challenges of Motivated Reasoning and Misinformation," *American Educational Research Journal*, Vol. 54, No. 1, 2017, pp. 11–12.

[65] Kahne and Bowyer, 2017, p. 15.

[66] Kahne and Bowyer, 2017, p. 25.

[67] Kahne and Bowyer, 2017, p. 6.

argue, and we agree, that future evaluations of specific interventions are necessary.[68]

Summary

In this chapter, we reviewed and provided examples of each of the tool types included in the database. We also described some of the research surrounding how each type of tool works and what we know about the effectiveness of different types of tools in countering disinformation and in helping information users make better decisions about their production and consumption of information. In the final chapter, we describe gaps within civil society efforts to counter disinformation and brainstorm about next steps for the field.

---

[68] Kahne and Bowyer, 2017, pp. 27–28.

CHAPTER FIVE

Conclusion

In this report, we have described a set of tools, developed by civil society organizations and nonprofits, that are aimed at countering online disinformation. We provide descriptive statistics on this universe of tools and then describe each category of tools in more depth, providing examples to illustrate different formats, methods, and delivery options for each category, along with a short review of what we know from existing research about how effective each type of tool is at combating disinformation. In this chapter, we synthesize key insights that emerge from the previous chapters; identify areas of promise, gaps, and future directions for this family of tools; and explore the role of civil society in the fight against disinformation more generally. We offer some recommendations for those who might wish to enter the field and/or develop new tools and for those considering investments to support new or existing tools.

Role of Civil Society

A starting point for an assessment of gaps and future directions of online tools developed by civil society organizations is a more general discussion about the ideal role of civil society organizations and nonprofits in the fight against disinformation. Although a full treatment of this question is outside the scope of this report, we offer a few thoughts here. Civil society organizations cannot step in for large tech and social media companies and take on the role those latter groups must play in stopping the spread of disinformation. Nor can civil society organizations replace appropriate governance mechanisms. Tech and social media companies, for example, have access to more resources and can use platform policies to influence incentives and directly address the flow of false and misleading information. Civil society organizations are also unlikely to ever replace media organizations in their ability to influence the spread of specific narratives or their ability to reach large audiences quickly. Finally, civil society and nonprofit groups cannot easily match the market power of for-profit companies or their ability to provide products to corporations and other large organizations in the area of disinformation.

Despite all of this, civil society organizations can play an important and leading role in the fight against disinformation in a few areas. First, they can reach audiences underserved by other actors. Civil society organizations' tools are free and generally easy to access, download, or install. Tech and social media companies have thus far failed to provide this type of tool; large private companies typically offer products that are too expensive or aimed at institutional clients. Second, civil society organizations are more agile and responsive than some larger corporations and have already filled the market with tools that tackle the disinformation challenges faced by the average user, even as larger companies and other organizations have moved at a slower pace. Third, these tools are innovative and experimental. Developers on the civil society side have been pioneering ways to use new technologies to assist users in their search for accurate information, and they continue to come up with new products, games, and tools to tackle the problem. This is one reason the field is growing and changing at such an active rate. Certainly, larger for-profit companies, tech companies, and other actors in this field have the ability to innovate—but civil society organizations have proven remarkably effective at developing new ideas, tools, and methods.

In terms of substance, civil society tools seem to fall into two main categories. The first set focuses on remediation: These tools address disinformation that has already infected the information system and typically work by identifying disinformation and flagging or correcting it. The second set of tools focuses on preventing the creation and spread of disinformation by improving the process through which information is generated and shared online. This set includes education and training products that aim to produce more-savvy information sharers, users, and consumers. Both prevention and remediation are natural places for civil society organizations to focus their efforts, and both types of efforts are needed in the fight against online disinformation. Having tools that can prevent the dissemination of false information is essential—and, in an ideal world, might be the preferred method of intervention because it prevents false information from ever entering the information ecosystem. However, because disinformation is already widespread and because we cannot realistically expect even the best prevention mechanisms to preempt all disinformation from entering the ecosystem, tools aimed at targeting disinformation after dissemination will be just as important.

Finally, the tools described target disinformation at two levels. One set focuses on the information itself—flagging the false information, tracking it, demoting its prevalence, or otherwise improving the quality of available information. The other set focuses on the information consumer—intending to provide signposts, guides, and mechanisms to inoculate information consumers against the effect of disinformation (or at least facilitate their efforts to avoid disinformation). These are complementary approaches, and both are necessary in overcoming the challenge of disinformation in the future.

Future Directions and Gaps to Be Addressed

Our review of tools highlights several gaps and priority areas of growth and investments when it comes to the field of online, civil society–developed tools to counter disinformation.

Need for Rigorous Evaluations

Throughout our review of tools, we were interested in finding objective evaluations of the extent to which the tools identified in our database had been proven effective in the fight against disinformation. In general, these evaluations were not publicly available. Although it is certainly possible that some organizations conduct their own internal evaluations, we were not able to locate many in the public domain. The assessment information we could find often involved output metrics (e.g., numbers of visitors) or other types of qualitative review. Ideally, investment dollars, grants, and contributions to civil society organizations working to counter disinformation should be allocated based on efficacy. Tools that prove reliable in countering the spread of disinformation or improving individual resilience to disinformation should be the ones to receive continued funding and support. Without metrics to assess the performance and effectiveness of a given tool, funders are left without objective criteria on which to make investment decisions.

To address this gap, civil society tools profiled in this database should be rigorously evaluated using randomized control trials and longitudinal analysis, wherever possible. This will be time-consuming, and it could take years to determine which tools have lasting effects. However, near-term assessments that measure performance before and after adoption of a tool or that compare users with nonusers (with needed controls) can provide initial diagnostics on what types of methods seem to be most effective as researchers and educators work toward more-sophisticated evaluations. Evaluations of this sort will be costly, but the information that they will provide to funders and to users selecting among different tools will be immeasurable. One possible investment approach for philanthropic organizations and private individuals seeking to counter disinformation could be to fund high-quality evaluations of existing tools. Such an investment could then inform the future direction of the field as subsequent investment could be allocated toward types of tools or specific tools that, based on objective data, seem to hold the most promise as counters to disinformation.

Aside from cost, it is worth acknowledging that there are other obstacles to conducting rigorous evaluations of the tools in this database. First, many are not user-friendly, and even those that are fully operational might lack the usability of commercial software, which could complicate the ability to assess performance or outcomes. Second, tools might appeal differently to different audiences. Many of the tools in the database are intended to appeal to diverse audiences; this could complicate the creation of a "real-world setting" for an evaluation.

Invest in Automation and Applications
One of the biggest obstacles that civil society organizations encounter when developing tools to counter online disinformation is their inabil-

ity to scale the tool—to get a sufficiently large population of people to use the tool and then to develop the capability needed to support the tool at a larger scale. Our database identifies a couple dozen types of verification tools, numerous education and training tools, multiple credibility-scoring tools, and a handful of others. When it comes to expanding the field from this base, especially with the evaluative metrics described previously, it is not clear that continuing to invest in new tools is the most efficient approach. First, having one or two more fact-checking technologies or one more bot detector might not significantly change the state of the field or advance the fight against disinformation. Second, even if there are specific ways in which the tools in this database could be improved (or specific types of tools that are significantly more effective than others), we do not have the full set of data needed to identify areas where improvement is most needed to achieve desired outcomes.

Instead, one productive set of investments might focus on supporting the ability of existing tools to reach and serve larger audiences by focusing on expanding delivery methods and committing to automation. The ability of a tool to increase its scale and reach will depend on accessibility and usability. The tools in our database had three primary modes of delivery—websites, browser extensions, and apps. Only a small number of tools used mobile apps. Yet, given the increasing shift of information dissemination and consumption toward the mobile format, mobile technologies might be the most scalable—and the easiest and most appealing for consumers to access and use. Mobile apps are highly portable and easily integrated into the information consumption habits of users. Investments focused on the development of mobile applications for existing verification, credibility-scoring, disinformation tracking, and other tools might therefore increase the user base of key tools. The development of apps or tablet versions of tools also might make these tools more appealing to teachers and for classroom use.

However, not all tools can be developed into apps (at least, not yet). Although greater use of mobile applications is promising, it will not be a cure-all. Alongside a focus on developing applications, tool developers might want to think about other ways to expand delivery—for example, partnerships to build certain tools into web browsers, easier access to a menu of possible extensions, and even partnerships across tools that might combine user bases. In addition, the development of a mobile app might not address the largest hurdle for many tools, which is simply awareness. Accessibility is one way to address scale; another would be to focus on marketing and advertisements. This might be a productive use of philanthropic dollars for more-promising tools.

Furthermore, the ability of a civil society organization to support an expanded user base is dependent on the method used by the tool. Human implementation, although simple in many ways, is not very scalable because humans can work only so fast and for so many hours. Verification tools that rely on human implementation, for instance, are limited by the number of fact-checks their employees can do on a given day. Other methods, such as machine learning, AI, crowdsourcing, and blockchain can be much more scalable because they are either automated or less labor intensive. However, these technologies remain somewhat undeveloped as applied to online tools. For example, although machine learning and AI have been applied to some extent to support verification tools, accuracy of such tools could be improved. Similarly, efforts to automate the tracking of disinformation and the scoring of sources based on credibility have not been widely exploited by existing tools. Across the field, for such technologies as machine learning, AI, crowdsourcing, and blockchain, improvements in accuracy, delivery, ease of use, and reliability would be valuable and could support a more widespread user base in the fight against disinformation. Investments that increase automation of existing tools or the development of new tools that exploit AI and other scalable methods could, therefore, advance the field across tool types and would be a good use of funds in the absence of more-objective data on what works or does not.

As a final note, although we focus here on scalability because it is ultimately a goal for many of the tools in our database, it is worth noting that not all tools are designed to be scalable. More-specialized tools designed to be used by educators, journalists, or other niche communities might not be scaled or even intended to be scaled, but they are still extremely valuable.

References

Adblock Plus, version 3.7, October 22, 2019. As of January 6, 2020:
https://adblockplus.org

Allcott, Hunt, Matthew Gentzkow, and Chuan Yu, "Trends in the Diffusion of Misinformation on Social Media," *Research & Politics*, Vol. 6, No. 2, April-June 2019, pp. 1–8.

Armbrust, Lloyd, Eric Oetker, Jonathan Dawe, April Halasz, and Zach Beasley, *Bitpress: News on the Blockchain*, Bitpress, March 10, 2018. As of October 7, 2019:
https://bitpress.news/assets/bitpress-whitepaper.pdf

Atlantic Council, "Why Should We Care About Disinformation?" YouTube, June 9, 2017. As of November 5, 2019:
https://www.youtube.com/watch?v=bLa89K8hJ_8

Baron, Sandra, and Rebecca Crootof, *Fighting Fake News: Workshop Report*, New Haven, Conn.: Information Society Project, The Floyd Abrams Institute for Freedom of Expression, Yale Law School, undated. As of November 4, 2019:
https://law.yale.edu/sites/default/files/area/center/isp/documents/fighting_fake_news_-_workshop_report.pdf

Berger, J. M., "The Methodology of the Hamilton 68 Dashboard," Alliance for Securing Democracy, August 7, 2017. As of November 4, 2019:
https://securingdemocracy.gmfus.org/the-methodology-of-the-hamilton-68-dashboard/

Bitpress, "The Fingerprint for Misinformation," webpage, undated-a. As of November 4, 2019:
https://bitpress.news/about/

———, "Our Process," webpage, undated-b. As of November 4, 2019:
https://bitpress.news/about/process/

Botcheck.me, "Detect & Track Twitter Bots," webpage, undated. As of November 4, 2019:
https://botcheck-website-dot-surfsafe-rbl.appspot.com

Botometer, homepage, undated. As of November 3, 2019:
https://botometer.iuni.iu.edu/#!/

BotSlayer, homepage, undated. As of December 9, 2019:
https://osome.iuni.iu.edu/tools/botslayer/

Citizen Evidence Lab, "About & FAQ," webpage, undated. As of November 4, 2019:
https://citizenevidence.org/about/

———, "YouTube Data Viewer," webpage, July 1, 2014. As of November 4, 2019:
https://citizenevidence.org/2014/07/01/youtube-dataviewer/

Clement, Scott, and Callum Borchers, "Facebook Plans to Crowdsource Media Credibility. This Chart Shows Why That Will Be So Difficult," *Washington Post*, January 24, 2018. As of September 17, 2019:
https://www.washingtonpost.com/news/the-fix/wp/2018/01/24/
facebook-plans-to-crowdsource-media-credibility-this-chart-shows-why-that-will-be-so-difficult/?utm_term=.dd960d2aeb7d

Constine, Josh, "Disrupt Hackathon App Notim.Press/Ed Algorithmically Detects Fake News," *TechCrunch*, December 4, 2016. As of September 17, 2019:
https://techcrunch.com/2016/12/04/not-impressed/

Curry, Alex, and Natalie Jomini Stroud, *Trust in Online News*, University of Texas at Austin, Center for Media Engagement, December 12, 2017. As of November 4, 2019:
https://mediaengagement.org/wp-content/uploads/2017/12/
CME-Trust-in-Online-News.pdf

Eigeman, Anne, "Trust Project Goes Independent to Help Public Distinguish News from Nonsense," *Nonprofit Quarterly*, June 4, 2019. As of November 4, 2019:
https://nonprofitquarterly.org/
trust-project-goes-independent-to-help-public-distinguish-news-from-nonsense/

FactCheck.org, "Our Process," webpage, May 3, 2019. As of September 17, 2019:
https://www.factcheck.org/our-process/

FakerFact, "About FakerFact," webpage, undated-a. As of November 4, 2019:
https://www.fakerfact.org/about

———, "How to Use Fakerfact," webpage, undated-b. As of September 26, 2019:
https://www.fakerfact.org/how-to-use

First Draft, "Education Area," webpage, undated-a. As of September 17, 2019:
https://firstdraftnews.org/en/education/curriculum-resource/
verifying-photos-videos/

———, "Verification Toolbox," webpage, undated-b. As of September 17, 2019:
https://firstdraftnews.org/verification-toolbox/

Fryling, Kevin, "How to Slay a Bot," *Science Node*, September 22, 2019. As of December 9, 2019:
https://sciencenode.org/feature/Botslayer.php

Hoaxy, "FAQ Index," webpage, undated. As of November 4, 2019:
https://hoaxy.iuni.iu.edu/faq.php#faq-q10

Holan, Angie Drobnic, "The Principles of the Truth-O-Meter: PolitiFact's Methodology for Independent Fact-Checking," *Politifact*, February 12, 2018. As of October 1, 2019:
https://www.politifact.com/truth-o-meter/article/2018/feb/12/
principles-truth-o-meter-politifacts-methodology-i/
#How%20we%20choose%20claims

Huguet, Alice, Jennifer Kavanagh, Garrett Baker, and Marjory S. Blumenthal, *Exploring Media Literacy Education as a Tool for Mitigating Truth Decay*, Santa Monica, Calif.: RAND Corporation, RR-3050-RC, 2019. As of November 03, 2019:
https://www.rand.org/pubs/research_reports/RR3050.html

Kahne, Joseph, and Benjamin Bowyer, "Educating for Democracy in a Partisan Age: Confronting the Challenges of Motivated Reasoning and Misinformation," *American Educational Research Journal*, Vol. 54, No. 1, 2017, pp. 3–34.

Kahneman, Daniel, and Shane Frederick, "Representativeness Revisited: Attribute Substitution in Intuitive Judgment," in Thomas Gilovich, Dale Griffin, and Daniel Kahneman, eds., *Heuristics and Biases: The Psychology of Intuitive Judgment*, Cambridge: Cambridge University Press, 2002, pp. 49–81.

Kavanagh, Jennifer, and Michael D. Rich, *Truth Decay: An Initial Exploration of the Diminishing Role of Facts and Analysis in American Public Life*, Santa Monica, Calif.: RAND Corporation, RR-2314-RC, 2018. As of January 6, 2020:
https://www.rand.org/pubs/research_reports/RR2314.html

Lapowsky, Issie, "This Browser Extension Is Like an Antivirus for Fake Photos," *Wired*, August 20, 2018. As of October 8, 2019:
https://www.wired.com/story/
surfsafe-browser-extension-save-you-from-fake-photos/

Maheshwari, Sapna, "Chase Had Ads on 400,000 Sites. Then on Just 5,000. Same Results," *New York Times*, March 29, 2017. As of October 3, 2019:
https://www.nytimes.com/2017/03/29/business/chase-ads-youtube-fake-news-offensive-videos.html

Media Bias/Fact Check, "Politifact," webpage, August 12, 2018. As of August 19, 2019:
https://mediabiasfactcheck.com/politifact/

Melford, Clare, Alexandra Mousavizadeh, and Danny Rogers, "A Global Disinformation Index—A Step in the Right Direction," *Medium*, April 12, 2018. As of September 17, 2019:
https://medium.com/@cmelford/
a-global-disinformation-index-a-step-in-the-right-direction-5165aee90198

Mustafaraj, Eni, and Panagiotis Metaxas, "The Fake News Spreading Plague: Was It Preventable?" *Proceedings of the ACM Web Science*, Troy, N.Y., 2017.

NewsGuard, homepage, undated. As of November 4, 2019:
https://www.newsguardtech.com/

Nyhan, Brendan, and Jason Reifler, "When Corrections Fail: The Persistence of Political Misperceptions," *Political Behavior*, Vol. 32, No. 2, June 2010, pp. 303–330.

———, *Misinformation and Fact-Checking: Research Findings from Social Science*, Media Policy Institute, February 2012. As of November 4, 2019:
https://pdfs.semanticscholar.org/93b3/
7d7c09100a443c4522b3392294bb1d8ae8bc.pdf?_ga=
2.222991391.527964909.1572893885-696852752.1572893885

Ostermeier, Eric, "Selection Bias? PolitiFact Rates Republican Statements as False at 3 Times the Rate of Democrats," *Smart Politics*, February 10, 2011. As of November 4, 2019:
https://editions.lib.umn.edu/smartpolitics/2011/02/10/selection-bias-politifact-rate/

Pennycook, Gordon, and David G. Rand, "Fighting Misinformation on Social Media Using Crowdsourced Judgments of News Source Quality," *PNAS*, Vol. 116, No. 7, 2019, pp. 2521–2526.

Pro-Truth Pledge, homepage, undated. As of November 4, 2019:
https://www.protruthpledge.org/

Radware, "Stop Bots in Real-Time with ShieldSquare Anti-Bot Solution," webpage, 2019. As of November 4, 2019:
https://www.shieldsquare.com/detect-and-block-bot-traffic/
?gclid=CjwKCAjw4avaBRBPEiwA_ZetYuZx2HIgkCCapCQ4Jt7gJAxdEfxmS0S
Ri0wwKLR8rFXY-swOrFJfUBoCkFwQAvD_BwE

RAND Corporation, "Fighting Disinformation Online: A Database of Web Tools," webpage, 2019. As of January 8, 2020:
https://www.rand.org/research/projects/truth-decay/fighting-disinformation.html

Reid, Alastair, "7 Vital Browser Plugins for Newsgathering and Verification," First Draft, August 26, 2016. As of September 17, 2019:
https://firstdraftnews.org/5-vital-browser-plugins-for-newsgathering-and-
verification-journalism-social-media/

Robb, Drew, "Whitelisting: Why and How It Works," *eSecurity Planet*, September 24, 2014. As of September 17, 2019:
https://www.esecurityplanet.com/malware/whitelisting-why-and-how-it-works.html

RoBhat Labs, homepage, undated. As of November 3, 2019:
https://www.robhat.com/#Work

Schafer, Bret, "Hamilton 2.0 Methodology and FAQs," Alliance for Securing Democracy, September 3, 2019. As of October 1, 2019:
https://securingdemocracy.gmfus.org/hamilton-2-0-methodology-faqs/

Share the Facts, "About," webpage, undated. As of September 17, 2019:
http://www.sharethefacts.org/about

Silverman, Craig, "Amnesty International Launches Video Verification Tool, Website," Poynter, July 8, 2014. As of October 2, 2019:
https://www.poynter.org/reporting-editing/2014/amnesty-international-launches-video-verification-tool-website/

Snopes, "About Us," webpage, undated. As of November 4, 2019:
https://www.snopes.com/about-snopes/

Sweney, Mark, "Vodafone to Stop Its Ads Appearing on Fake News and Hate Speech Sites," *The Guardian*, June 6, 2017. As of September 17, 2019:
https://www.theguardian.com/business/2017/jun/06/vodafone-ads-fake-news-hate-speech-google-facebook-advertising

Thomas, Laurel, "U-M Tool Measures 'Iffy' News on Social Media in Time for 2018 Election," *Michigan News*, University of Michigan, October 10, 2018. As of September 10, 2019:
https://news.umich.edu/u-m-tool-measures-iffy-news-on-social-media-in-time-for-2018-election/

Thomsen, Jacqueline, "Researchers Unveil Tool to Track Disinformation on Social Media," *The Hill*, October 10, 2018. As of September 17, 2019:
https://thehill.com/policy/cybersecurity/410651-researchers-unveil-tool-tracking-disinformation-being-shared-on-social

Tsipursky, Gleb, "The Pro-Truth Pledge: An Effective Strategy for Skeptics to Fight Fake News and Post-Truth Politics," *Skeptic*, undated. As of November 4, 2019:
https://www.skeptic.com/reading_room/take-pro-truth-pledge-fight-fake-news/

Tsipursky, Gleb, Fabio Votta, and Kathryn M. Roose, "Fighting Fake News and Post-Truth Politics with Behavioral Science: The Pro-Truth Pledge," *Behavior and Social Issues*, Vol. 27, 2018, pp. 47–70.

Trust Project, "Frequently Asked Questions," webpage, undated. As of September 17, 2019:
https://thetrustproject.org/faq/#indicator

Trusted Times, "How to Use Trusted Times," webpage, undated. As of November 4, 2019:
https://trustedtimes.org/how-to-use-trusted-times/

USAFacts, "About Us," webpage, undated-a. As of September 17, 2019:
https://usafacts.org/about

———, homepage, undated-b. As of September 17, 2019:
https://usafacts.org/

Varol, Onur, Emilio Ferrara, Clayton A. Davis, Filippo Menczer, and Alessandro Flammini, "Online Human-Bot Interactions: Detection, Estimation, and Characterization," *Proceedings of the Eleventh International AAAI Conference on Web and Social Media*, 2017.

Verification Handbook, homepage, undated. As of September 17, 2019:
http://verificationhandbook.com/

Walter, Nathan, Jonathan Cohen, R. Lance Holbert, and Yasmin Morag, "Fact-Checking: A Meta-Analysis of What Works and for Whom," *Political Communication*, 2019, pp. 1–26.

Webb, Theresa, and Kathryn Martin, "Evaluation of a US School-Based Media Literacy Violence Prevention Curriculum on Changes in Knowledge and Critical Thinking Among Adolescents," *Journal of Children and Media*, Vol. 6, No. 4, 2012, pp. 430–449.

Website Whitelist, version 6.2.3, May 12, 2018. As of January 6, 2020:
https://chrome.google.com/webstore/detail/website-whitelist/bmlipnlhfpjgmafjlnnmdkldjmcbahnm?hl_en

Wojcik, Stefan, Solomon Messing, Aaron Smith, Lee Rainie, and Paul Hitlin, "Bots in the Twittersphere," Pew Research Center, April 9, 2018. As of November 3, 2019:
https://www.pewresearch.org/internet/2018/04/09/bots-in-the-twittersphere/

Yang, Kai-Cheng, Onur Varol, Clayton A. Davis, Emilio Ferrara, Alessandro Flammini, and Filippo Menczer, "Arming the Public with Artificial Intelligence to Counter Social Bots," *Human Behavior & Emerging Technology*, Vol. 1, No. 1, 2019, pp. 48–61.